Quiet Fire

A Historical

Anthology of

Asian American

Poetry

1892–1970

THE ASIAN AMERICAN WRITERS' WORKSHOP • NEW YORK

QUIET FIRE:

A HISTORICAL ANTHOLOGY OF

ASIAN AMERICAN POETRY 1892–1970

© 1996 by Juliana Chang
Library of Congress Number 96-78961
ISBN 1-889876-02-x

Design by Wendy Lee
Cover art by Daviko Marcel,
photographed by David Carras
Distributed by Rutgers University Press
Printed in the United States of America

This publication is made possible by a grant from the Witter Bynner Foundation for Poetry. The Asian American Writers' Workshop is a not-for-profit literary organization devoted to the creation, development and dissemination of Asian American literature, and is supported by the National Endowment for the Arts, the New York Sate Council on the Arts, the Department of Cultural Affairs, Jerome Foundation, Bay Foundation, Greenwall Foundation, Axe Houghton Foundation, New York Foundation for the Arts, AT & T, Anheuser-Busch, Avon Corporation, Consolidated Edison, and Two St. Marks Corporation.

FOR MY PARENTS,

Victor Fong-Shou Chang &

Mary Mei-Lee Chu Chang

CONTENTS

ACKNOWLEDGMENTS

I thank Curtis Chin of the Asian American Writers Workshop for first conceiving of this project, for finding support for it, and for his assistance and understanding throughout. Thanks to the Witter Bynner Foundation for Poetry for their generous support, as well as the Boston College Undergraduate Fellows Program for funding research assistance. I am grateful to my interns and assistants Kathleen Hunvirapunth, Helen Mah, Michelle Lee, Karen Hom, Candace Nakagawa, and especially Nisha Chatani, Rose Cha and Cathy Hong. Thanks also to Eric Gamalinda at the Writers Workshop, who saw through the completion of this project.

Walter K. Lew patiently read over several versions of the manuscript, giving me valuable and constant feedback throughout the entire project. He also compiled and edited the appended essays on the recent histories of Asian American poetry. Both Walter and Brian Kim Stefans helped me to reconceptualize the historical aspects of this anthology. I thank Brian for his detailed and thought-provoking feedback on the manuscript, and his suggestions of several pieces by Sadakichi Hartmann. Christine So, James Kyung-Jin Lee, Amy Yang, and Victor Bascara also gave helpful feedback. Monique H.D. Truong, Craig Huynh, and Viet Nguyen gave me leads for sources of Vietnamese American poetry; since the temporal scope of the anthology has changed, I am regretfully unable to use these sources. Steven Doi gave me access to several rare books, for which I am very grateful. Juliana Koo provided information on obtaining permissions-to-reprint. Richard Ehara introduced me to the work of Daviko Marcel, who provided the cover art.

Thanks are also due to Sharon Lim-Hing, Shirley Geok-lin Lim, Kimiko Hahn, Jessica Hagedorn, George Uba, Eric Chock, Maria Hong, Shawn Wong, and Eri Yasuhara, for suggestions; Fred Ho, Russell Leong, Lawson Inada and Alan Chong Lau made especially detailed suggestions. I thank Russell for introducing me to the writing of Charles Yu.

I gratefully acknowledge the bibliographical work of King-kok Cheung and Stan Yogi, whose *Asian American Literature: An Annotated Bibliography* helped guide my research.

Finally, many thanks to the countless people who talked to the interns at the Writers Workshop looking for possible contact information for the writers in this anthology. Responsibility for the final selection of poems, including any oversights and omissions, is mine alone.

I N T R O D U C T I O N :
On Recovering Asian American Poetry

"I have sat up all night, convinced
that something is being asked
to be recovered, that somewhere
an old doorway in the earth is opening,
releasing what I've lost. And yet
as I reach forward to turn off the lamp
and the room fills with quiet fire
and pigeons scuffle on the window sill,
I don't know. I don't know."
                    -Patricia Y. Ikeda, "Recovery"

This compilation of Asian American poetry from 1892
to 1970 recovers Asian American poetic history, a recovery
that acts "against amnesia," in Adrienne Rich's phrase. The
dominant, selective construction of U.S. literary history has
rendered writers of color either "minor" or invisible, cutting
off contemporary writers and readers from Asian American
poetic histories, traditions, legacies. This anthology is
intended to serve as an archival counter-memory, illuminating
the gaps in what has been presented as "American poetry"
and "American culture." Asian American literature is often
assumed to be a recently invented and individualistic
phenomenon; contemporary critics and readers may believe
that Asian American poetic writing originated in recent
volumes of poetry by individual critically-lauded writers.
Against this assumption, and against what David Palumbo-
Liu calls "the fetishization of the present" in Asian American
literary studies, I would like to briefly recuperate the history
of Asian American poetic discourse. In the following
summary, my movement back through time is meant to
show that for each commonly-assumed moment of origin,
there is often in fact a previous moment.

Asian American poetry did not begin in the late 1980s,
when David Mura's *After We Lost Our Way* was selected
for the National Poetry Series in 1989 and Garrett Hongo

and Li-Young Lee were awarded the Lamont Poetry Prize in 1987 and 1990, respectively. Nor did it begin: in the early 1980s, when Cathy Song's *Picture Bride* received the Yale Younger Series of Poets Award in 1982, John Yau's *Corpse and Mirror* was selected for the National Poetry Series in 1983, and Joseph Bruchac edited *Breaking Silence: An Anthology of Contemporary Asian-American Poets* in 1983; in the late 1970s, when special issues of journals such as *Greenfield Review* (1977) and *Sunbury* (1979) highlighted Asian American poetic writing, and prominent feminist poets Mitsuye Yamada and Janice Mirikitani published their first volumes, *Camp Notes and Other Poems* (1976) and *Awake in the River* (1978), respectively; in the early 1970s, when poetic writing was included in several pioneering Asian American anthologies, including Amy Tachiki, *et al.'s Roots: An Asian American Reader* (1971); Kai-yu Hsu and Helen Palubinskas' *Asian-American Authors* (1972); Frank Chin *et al's Aiiieeeee! An Anthology of Asian-American Writings* (1974); and David Hsin-fu Wand's *Asian American Heritage: An Anthology of Prose and Poetry* (1974), as well as more ethnically specific (e.g., *Liwanag*, a Filipino American publication) or multiracial (e.g., *Time to Greez!*, cited above) or campus-based publications. While these each signify important moments in the history of Asian American poetry, the trajectory of Asian American poetic discourse extends even further back.

Asian American poetry dates as far back as the 1890s, with the publication of poems by Sadakichi Hartmann, considered among the first to write Symbolist poetry in English, and Yone Noguchi, whose work interested his well-known contemporaries Willa Cather, Thomas Hardy, and George Meredith. Hartmann served as a secretary to Walt Whitman, and had the dubious distinction of being referred to by Whitman once as "that damn Japanee." Whitman's poetic influence can be clearly seen in Noguchi's long lines and grand cosmic vision. The poet Joaquin Miller was a mentor to Noguchi, and an influence on Takashi Kanno (not in this anthology). In addition to poetry in its written and published form, this anthology considers nontraditional oral and written forms as poetic discourse: we can date Japanese folksong-derived plantation worksongs (hole-hole bushi), Cantonese rhymes from Chinatown collected by Marlon K. Hom, and poems carved on the walls of the Angel Island detaining station (Lai, Lim, and Yung) to the first decades of the twentieth century. One plantation worksong describes how the laborers end up literally putting in roots, physically becoming part of the land they work on: "Those who came on the First and Second ships/And still don't go back home to Japan,/Will become fertilizer at the end/For the poi plants." Despite this physical mingling with the land, Asian Americans have been peculiarly racialized as inherently foreign to the United States. This status of being outside national boundaries is ironically inscribed by the forced confinement of Asian emigrants in detaining stations, as lamented in some of the Cantonese rhymes and the Angel Island poems. H.T. Tsiang published his Marxist-internationalist poetry in 1929, as well as the experimental proletarian narrative The Hanging in Union Square in 1935. Tsiang's "Chinaman, Laundryman" and Wen I-to's "The Laundry Song" depict the rhythms of racialized labor, the bodily fluids of blood, sweat and tears signifying the hardship of labor.

Regional haiku, tanka, and senryu societies were particularly active in the early and mid-twentieth century; excerpts from Nixon and Tana's collection *Sounds from the Unknown* provide a sampling of writing from this milieu. Toyo Suyemoto's skillfully crafted rhymed verses were published first in magazines such as *Current Life* (as were Hisaye Yamamoto's), and then in the Japanese American internment camp journals of the 1940s. Around this period, Jose Garcia Villa and Carlos Bulosan each published highly distinctive poetic work. Bulosan's writing focuses mainly on proletarian life, labor, and politics. Villa's work was considered "mystic" in its descriptions of religious ecstacy. One cluster of Villa's poetry was striking in its experimentation with punctuation. Edith Sitwell called Villa's defamiliarization of language "beautiful and strange." Notable writers who wrote or published their first poems in the 1960s include Fred Wah, Joy Kogawa, Jessica Hagedorn, and Lawson Inada. Kogawa, best known in Asian American literary circles for her novel *Obasan*, has in fact published several volumes of poetry. Wah's poetic and editorial work is highly regarded in Canada, under-recognized in the United States. Hagedorn and Inada continue the mapping of the U.S. urban landscape begun in Sadakichi Hartmann's "To the 'Flat-Iron'" in their sharply satiric ethnic and racial vernacular renderings of San Francisco and West Fresno. The selections in this anthology give a sense of this Asian American poetic history, a history that contemporary readers and writers can draw from.

• • • • • •

Contemporary poet Patricia Ikeda's "Recovery" provides the epigraph to this essay. In this poem as well as her poem "Translations" (both in Bruchac's *Breaking Silence*), fire is the powerful force that destroys traces of history, leading to the subject's sense of both loss and desire. But fire also represents potential, "the spark/of a struck flint" ("Recovery"), illumination, a powerful radiation.

The speaker in Toyo Suyemoto's "Dusk," sharpens her vision at night; searching in the darkness to discover what has been obscured and lost. "But I shall look into the dark/For some lost star." Carlos Bulosan similarly evokes men and women "searching/in the pages of history for the lost word." Meanwhile, Masao Handa writes of using a "fire within" as illumination, to guide him in the darkness as he searches for an "other self," perhaps a mate or a fellow Japanese American. All three poets describe a quest for something precious, lost or hidden. But Fred Wah suggests that we will encounter fire, even when we least intend it: "What I had expected/was to sleep for the ride with eyes closed/not drive into a burning mountainside." The speaker is originally complacent, planning to sleep through his journey; instead, he ends up driving directly into fire, the bright orange glow of the sky contrasting with the pitch black he anticipates. Using fire as a figure for history, I read the poem as an allegorical cautionary tale: even those that would deny the significance of racial history must inevitably confront the history of racial formation in North America, a history that affects literary canon formation.

In "57," Jose Garcia Villa's poem of religious rapture, the encounter with God is compared to a flaming explosion, "sparks flying till I was all/Embers." The speaker is instructed then to return to the earthly realm now that "Understanding is [his]," but is told to "Beware: beware! since [he] and God have lovered." The speaker, having stolen the fire of knowledge, has transgressed the divide between mortal and immortal, his state of knowledge ecstatic and dangerous. In contrast, Wong May presents the limits of our knowledge of celestial fire. In "Bastard," the sun is a godlike egg, self-begotten, perpetually hatching itself. "The sun/has been hatching itself/for God knows/how many years..." In our human life span, "we will not live to see it" finally burn out.

I take Villa's and Wong's poems as two poles: our desires and our limitations in the face of fire--the simultaneous destruction and illumination of history. In my research for this anthology, I was constantly confronted with the spectre of lost history: how many copies of these fragile, dusty books were left in the world? How could we begin to find out about some of the more obscure poets, whose books were published by small presses that have long since vanished? How are these pieces relics of a now-gone life and history? How do we read, in the present, these remains of the past? This collection provides some traces and remnants that I hope will prove illuminating of an Asian American poetic history.

• • • • • •

I end the selection of poems at 1970 for several reasons. Increased Asian immigration resulting from liberalized immigration laws in 1965, as well as the historic Asian American political and cultural movements of the 1960s and 1970s, resulted in the emergence of new cultural configurations during this period. 1971 is the publication date of two seminal texts whose context is the incipient formation of a politicized Asian American collective consciousness. *Roots: An Asian American Reader*, and Lawson Inada's *Before the War: Poems as they happened*, as publications that articulate this ethnic and racial consciousness, mark the beginning of a new era in Asian American studies and Asian American poetry. The subsequent period was one in which Asian American publications blossomed, as alluded to above. 1971 is also the beginning of the period that Fay Chiang writes about in her essay about New York City's Basement Workshop in the appendix. The appended essays by Chiang, Eric Chock, Alan Chong Lau, Gerry Shikatani and Kimiko Hahn (compiled and edited by Walter K. Lew) provide an overview of Asian American poetry movements for the past twenty-five years. For collections of contemporary Asian American poetry, see the anthologies *Breaking Silence: An Anthology of Contemporary Asian-American Poets*, ed. Joseph Bruchac; *The Open Boat: Poems from Asian America*, ed. Garrett Hongo; and *Premonitions: The Kaya Anthology of New Asian North American Poetry*, ed. Walter K. Lew.

My project in compiling these works is to perform a preliminary act of recovery: unearthing obscured poetry that deserves wider recognition. However, this anthology is not meant to provide a comprehensive history of Asian American poetry; given its limitations in length, it could hardly do so. What is presented here is only a small sampling of what has been written or published. Many noteworthy poems had to be excluded because we could not afford permissions-to-reprint, or because we were unable to contact the writers or estates. The bibliography may be consulted for more sources of Asian American poetry. I hope that others will continue this research, especially in poetry composed in languages other than English, an area of study that deserves more acts of excavation and illumination.

SADAKICHI HARTMANN

Cyanogen Seas
Are Surging

Cyanogen seas are surging
On fierce cinnabarine strands,
Where white Amazons are marching,
Through the radiance of the sands.

Oh, could only lambent love-flame
Be like the surging sea,
Deluge the red of the desert
And drown the white virgins in me!

1892

SADAKICHI HARTMANN

Cathedral Sacrilege

A silken hose in a golden haze
An opening rose in a maze of lace
A color dream in marmorean whiteness
A sensual gleam in subdued brightness
　　And my languid soul
　　In a mild vibration
　　Embraces the nude
　　In a wild violation.

1892

SADAKICHI HARTMANN

Buddha: Scene XII
Darkness in Space

Poetical license imagines that, at BUDDHA's entering Nirvana, a color revery takes place in the universe. This scene, a concert of self-radiant colors, is to be represented by pyrotechny, brought by chemistry, electricity and future light-producing sciences to such perfection and beauty that it becomes the new Optic Art, in which Color will rival Sound as a vehicle of pure emotion.

SCENE: Bluish-black darkness in space: a minute section of the universe, represented by a stage of at least 800 yards length and 500 yards height and depth.

I. Out of darkness the earth, in the ban of the sun and followed by her paramour the moon, ever revolving rolls majestically forward, displaying the phenomena of a lunar and solar eclipse, and growing larger and larger until she has become so large that one can discern: the ultra-marine of the oceans, the glaucous of the steppes, the pallid gold of the deserts, the crystal fretwork of the poles and glaciers, and here and there the dark flyspecks of the largest cities, which become scintillant as the other colors fade in the earthly night. It impresses the beholder like the colossal ideal of human vanity and then rolls backwards into darkness.

II. Confused tumbling of meteors through space-a symbol of man's life, propelled from some unknown bourn and rushing to some unknown goal, proving its momentary existence merely by a luminous line, lit and extinguished without change of course. The meteors, varying continually in the rhythm of entrance and exit, mobility, richness and intensity of fire, shoot forth in every direction, also in every possible angle, towards the audience.

III. Incessant rain of luminous stellar dust, in the

midst of which a battle of stars, comets, planets with rings and satellites, take place. They rush towards each other, and recede, encircle each other and create endless variations of figures. Now and then stars crash into each other with a great explosion of fire, unite into larger stars and, continuing their course, emit a light produced by a combination of their colors when separate. Suddenly the stars grow larger and larger, the smaller ones disappearing behind the larger, until a few dozens have reached the diameter of 50 yards, who in turn repeat the crescendo of concussions. An orange and a blue star collide and form a still larger one radiating a greenish light of painful hope. A roseate and blue star also collide to a violet glow of melancholy bliss. Thereupon these two collide, and before they grow into one, all the other stars crush into them, causing an incandescent firebrand that radiates the entire space with its irisating light. This fire wall is suddenly cleft in two, and in innumerable hues and palpitations melts away in "diminuendo."

IV. The lower (1/4) part of the stage represents the sea of chaos over which by some caprice the light effects of an earthly day, from a blood red dawn to a moonlit night, are performed in color gradations of subtlest purity, accompanied by descriptive music.

Intermezzo, entitled "Alhambra Arabesques." In succession the famous patterns in luminous gold, blue, and faded red, interlace, overlap, and link each other before the eyes of the audience, and finally change into an improvisation of new designs of the same character. (For other intermezzos the author suggests "The Shattered Jewel Casket," "Flowers Growing in Cloudland," etc.)

V. A kaleidoscopical symphony of color effects continually changing in elation and depression, velocity, intensity, variety and sentiment, continually developing and composing new forms and designs, not merely of mathematical symmetry, but also as suggested from the endless constructions, textures, phenomena revealed in astronomy, microscopy, mineralogy, geology, paleontology, etc., beginning with a *Larghetto* in light bluish-grey, muddy yellowish-green, greenish-blue and dark greyish-blue; followed by an *Andante* in color containing blue from green to purple; by an *Allegretto* of complimentary colors with a tendency towards yellow and red; and by a *Finale vivace* in all colors, ending at last with a flower star, emitting rocket-like fire lines, trills, radiations of various propelling power, at first paraphrasing in the colors of the solar spectrum, and at last improvising an outburst of new colors, like ultra red and violet, for which optical instruments have first to be invented before the human eye can perceive and enjoy them.

1897

To the "Flat-Iron"

On roof and street, on park and pier
    The spring-tide sun shines soft and white,
Where the "Flat-iron," gaunt, austere,
    Lifts its huge tiers in limpid light.
      From the city's stir and madd'ning roar
    Your monstrous shape soars in massive flight;
And 'mid the breezes the ocean bore
    Your windows flare in the sunset light.
      Lonely and lithe, o'er the nocturnal
        City's flickering flame, you proudly tower,
      Like some ancient giant monolith,
        Girt with the stars and mists that lour.

      All else we see fade fast and disappear—
        Only your prow-like form looms gaunt, austere,
      As in a sea of fog, now veiled, now clear.

Iron structure of the time,
    Rich, in showing no pretense,
Frail, in frugalness sublime,
    Emblem staunch of common sense,
Well may you smile over Gotham's vast domain
    As dawn greets your pillars with roseate flame,
      For future ages will proclaim
        Your beauty
        Boldly, without shame.

1903

Tanka I

Winter? Spring! Who knows!
    White buds from the plumtrees wing
And mingle with the snows.
    No blue skies these flowers bring,
    Yet their fragrance augurs Spring.

1920

Tanka III

Moon, somnolent, white,
 Mirrored in a waveless sea,
What fickle mood of night
 Urged thee from heaven to flee
 And live in the dawnlit sea!

1920

YONE NOGUCHI

Seas of Loneliness

Underneath the void-colored shade of the trees, my
　　"self" passed as a drowsy cloud into Somewhere.
I see my soul floating upon the face of the deep, nay
　　the faceless face of the deepless deep—
Ah, the Seas of Loneliness!
The mute-waving, silence-waters, ever shoreless,
　　bottomless, heavenless, colorless, have no
　　shadow of my passing soul.
Alas, I, without wisdom, without foolishness,
　　without goodness, without badness,—am
　　like god, a negative god, at least!
Is that a quail? One voice out of the back-hill jumped
　　into the ocean of loneliness.
Alas, what sound resounds; what color returns; the
　　bottom, the heaven, too, reappears!
There is no place of muteness! Yea, my paradise is
　　lost in this moment!
I want not pleasure, sadness, love, hatred, success,
　　unsuccess, beauty, ugliness—only the mighty
　　Nothing in No More.

1896/7

Lines

The sun I worship,
Not for the light, but for the shadows of the trees he draws:
O shadows welcome like an angel's bower,
Where I build Summer-day dream!
Not for her love, but for the love's memory,
The woman I adore;
Love may die, but not the memory eternally green—
The well where I drink Spring ecstasy.
To a bird's song I listen,
Not for the voice, but for the silence following after the song:
O Silence fresh from the bosom of voice!—
Melody from the Death-Land whither my face does ever turn!

1909

In Japan Beyond

Do you not hear the sighing of a willow in Japan,
(In Japan beyond, in Japan beyond)
In the voice of a wind searching for the sun lost,
For the old faces with memory in eyes?

Do you not hear the sighing of a bamboo in Japan,
(In Japan beyond, in Japan beyond)
In the voice of a sea urging with the night,
For the old dreams of a twilight tale?

Do you not hear the sighing of a pine in Japan,
(In Japan beyond, in Japan beyond)
In the voice of a river in quest of the Unknown,
For the old ages with gold in heart?

Do you not hear the sighing of a reed in Japan,
(In Japan beyond, in Japan beyond)
In the voice of a bird who long ago flew away,
For the old peace with velvet-sandalled feet?

1909

To Robert Browning

You are a smoking-room story-teller of the pageant of
    life seen by senses,
Your gusto in speech turns your art into obscurity,
Again from the obscurity into valedictory:
You are a provincialism endorsed by eccentric pride.
You are sometimes riotous to escape from anarchism,
Your great thirst for expression makes you a
    soul-wounding romancer,
You often play the mystagogue, and appear cruel.
You are a glutton by colorful adventures,
You are a tronbadour serenading between the
    stars and life.
Your love song on a guitar torments us even physically;
You are a realist who under the darkness purifies
    himself into the light of optimism;
You are a griffin wildly dancing on human laughter.

1923

ANONYMOUS

Hole-Hole Bushi

Kane wa kachiken
Washa horehore yo
Ase to namida no
Tomokasegi

My husband cuts the cane,
I do the *hole hole*.
By sweat and tears
We get by.

Hawaii Hawaii to

Kite mirya Jigoku
Boshi ga Emma de
Runa ga oni

Wonderful Hawaii, or so I
heard.
One look and it seems like Hell.
The manager's the Devil and
His *lunas* are demons.

Dekasegi wa kuru kuru
Hawaii wa tsumaru
Ai no Nakayama

Kane ga furu

The laborers keep on coming
Overflowing these Islands
But it's only Inspector
Nakayama
Who rakes in the profits.

Sanjugosen no
Hore hore shiyo yori
Pake-san to moi-moi surya
Akahi kala

Why settle for 35¢
Doing *hole hole* all day,
When I can make a dollar
Sleeping with that *pake?*

(Translation: Franklin S. Odo and Harry Minorn Urata)

ANONYMOUS

Ikkai nikai de   Those who came on First and
                        Second ships
Kaeranu mono wa   And still don't go back home
                        to Japan,
Sue wa Hawai de   Will become fertilizer at
                        the end
Poi no koe   For the poi plants.

Sodo okoshite   If we can get married
Sowareru mi narya   By stirring up troubles,
Hayaku sodo ga   I'll like to start the troubles
Okoshitai   Very soon.

Asu wa Sande ja   Tomorrow is Sunday;
Asobi ni oide   Come and spend the
                        day with me.
Kane wa hanawai   My husband works but
                        I'll be home
Washa uchi ni   All alone.

ANONYMOUS

Tanomoshi otoshite
Wahine o yonde
Hito ni torarete

Beso kaita

I took the tanomoshi money
And got my wife from Japan.
But I blubbered so hard
when someone
Snatched her away.

Joyaku wa kirerushi
Miren wa nokoru
Danburo no wahine nya

Ki ga nokoru

The contract is over and yet
I hate to give up my work
If I do, I'll miss the
woman who lives
Outside the camp.

(Translation: Yukho Uyehara)

1885–1910

ANONYMOUS

From *Songs of Gold Mountain*

6

The wooden cell is like a steel barrel.
Firmly shut, not even a breeze can filter through.
Over a hundred cruel laws, hard to list them all;
Ten thousand grievances, all from the tortures
    day and night.
Worry, and more worry—
How can I sleep in peace or eat at ease?
There isn't a cangue, but the hidden punishment
    is just as weighty.
Tears soak my clothes; frustration fills my bosom.

1911

室板如鐵桶。嚴關不漏風。
百般苛例講唔窮(一)。朝夕被凌悲萬種。
憂忡忡。寢膳遑安用。
雖無枷鎖陰刑重。淚滿衣裳悶滿胸。

（一）唔窮：不盡

ANONYMOUS

10

The mighty power rescinds her treaty;
The weak race suffers oppression from the mighty.
I am jailed unjustly across the bay,
Enduring the unendurable tyranny of immigration oficials.
Doors: firmly shut.
Guards and officers: watching me closely, like wolves.
News and letters: not permitted.
O, it's hard to bear the hundred cruel regulations they
        devise at will.

1911

強權廢約例。弱種受他掣。
無辜困我隔江涯。關吏橫行眞譽抵(一)。
門緊閉。狼差嚴密睇(二)。
音信不容驛使遞。苛條百出確難捱。

(一)譽抵：難以抵受
(二)睇：監守
(三)苛條：指排華苛例

ANONYMOUS

29

Men on the remote frontier, all terrified:
In autumn, north winds begin to blow.
Sojourners from faraway places share the
    same thought:
O, how can this little bit of clothing be enough in
    deep frost and heavy snow?
Once winter comes—
A fur coat is needed all the more in the
    freezing cold.
I can buy one at a clothing store,
But it's not the same as the one sewn by my dear
    wife or my mother.

1915

遠塞人心悚。因秋起朔風(一)。
遐方旅客念相同。衫少怎當霜雪重。
一交冬。更需裘禦凍。
服店雖能加購用。爭如慈母與妻縫。

（一）當：作「擋」

57

Husband has gone to a country far away.
The sorrows of separation are manifold in kind.
The bedroom is desolate; the quilt, chilly.
How can a single pillow be my mate in
    my lonely sleep?
My restless sleep?
With emotions suspended, depression lingers on.
I am thinking of my man, who hasn't yet returned
    from the ends of the earth;
I look up, and the moon, so round and full, brings
    me insurmountable frustration.

1911

懷念天涯人未轉。舉頭惱煞月團圓。

睡不安。情牽難解悶。

羅幃寂靜嘆襟寒。孤枕獨眠誰作伴。

君適他邦遠。離愁幾百般。

137

What a batch of lousy broads,
All without proper upbringing.
They hustle in the doorways, their gold teeth
    on parade;
Day and night, always going to the picture show.
They are fearless.
They laugh with lust and speak the barbarian
    tongue.
With men, they are experts at fooling around.
Alas, their dissipation is shameful to our China.

1915

怎班爛尽姆(一)。概不入教化。
門前賣俏演金牙。朝夕時常睇影畫。
乜唔怕(二)。淫笑講番話(三)。
專與男人去遊耍。荒唐羞辱我中華。

(一) 爛尽姆：淫賤女子；責罵女性的粗俗台山方言

(二) 乜唔怕：什麼也不怕

(三) 番話：外國語，指英語

211

Trying to line up fun-loving johns,
They've changed their clothing styles.
Now they wear heels in whorehouses
Like the fad among school girls,
As if there's no longer a difference between the two.
Still, their skin and flesh are for hire.
If they don't follow the trends, people will be bored
And they might as well close up shop and
    take down their signs.

1915

想攬風流婿。轉過個身勢。(一)
娼寮皆著有踭鞋。形式相同學生派。(二)
似無制。仍然皮肉賣。
若不從新人厭睇。幾乎唔駛掛招牌。(三)

（一）身勢：外表（衣服）打扮
（二）娼寮：參看歌 #188
（三）唔駛：參看歌 #113

JUN FUJITA

To Elizabeth

Against the door dead leaves are falling;
On your window the cobwebs are black.
Today, I linger alone.

The foot-step?
A passer-by.

1923

Miriam

A sigh among the trees;
A sudden shower of large rain-drops—
I hear no voice, today.

On the wet grass
Paper, crumpled, flaps.

1923

JUN FUJITA

Michigan Boulevard

A row of black tombs—tall and jagged,
The buildings stand in the drizzly night.
With vacant stare the boulevard lamps in rain
Amuse the green gleams they cast.
Beyond the lamps, among the tombs,
Drip, and drip,
The hollow sound rises.

1923

JUN FUJITA

Chicago River

Slowly, by the slimy wooden wharves,
Through the stillness of rain
The Chicago River glides into the night.
From the silhouette of a black iron bridge,
The watchman's light is dripping-
Dripping like melting tallow.
Out of darkness
Comes a woman,
Hellos to me; her wet face glares;
Casually she turns and goes
Into the darkness.

Through the stillness of rain
The Chicago River glides on.

1923

WEN I-TO

The Laundry Song

(One piece, two pieces, three pieces,)
Washing must be clean.
(Four piece, five pieces, six pieces,)
Ironing must be smooth.

I can wash handkerchiefs wet with sad tears;
I can wash shirts soiled in sinful crimes.
The grease of greed, the dirt of desire...
And all the filthy things at your house,
Give them to me to wash, give them to me.

Brass stinks so; blood smells evil.
Dirty things you have to wash.
Once washed, they will again be soiled.
How can you, men of patience, ignore them!
Wash them (for the Americans), wash them!

You saythe laundry business is too base.
Only Chinamen are willing to stoop so low?
It was your preacher who once told me:
Christ's father used to be a carpenter.
Do you believe it? Don't you believe it?

There isn't much you can do with soap and water.
Washing clothes truly can't compare with building warships.
I, too, say what great prospect lies in this—
Washing the other's sweat with your own blood and sweat?
(But) do you want to do it? Do you want it?

Year in year out a drop of homesick tears;
Midnight, in the depth of night, a laundry lamp...
Menial or not, you need not bother,
Just see what is not clean, what is not smooth,
And ask the Chinaman, ask the Chinaman.

I can wash handkerchiefs wet with sad tears,
I can wash shirts soiled in sinful crimes.
The grease of greed, the dirt of desire...
And all the filthy things at your house,
Give them to me—I'll wash them, give them to me!

1925

MASAO HANDA

I Am a Firefly

I am a firefly
With a tiny lantern lighted.
In search of my other self,
In the darkness of night
I fly. Tired I bathe myself
In the falling dew.
The night speaks to me,
But alas! I do not understand;
Through the vastness of obscurity
I fly, in search of my other self.
I am a firefly
With a tiny lantern lighted.

1928

H.T. TSIANG

Shantung

Don, Don, Don, the drum is calling;
Lun, Lun, Lun, the artillery is roaring.
Japan is in Shantung, Shantung,
In Shanghai far away
We can still work for a living.

Hashi yi, hashi yi, buzzing bee, buzzing bee.
God has damned me,
Hard work comes to me.
My mouth is thirsty,
My stomach was never so empty,
Why don't you teach me to live without bread,
Papa, mama?

The whip is cracking,
The click is in my ear;
A look at the foreman's face
And my heart always blackens.
Think ye,
He can stop my tears, and my ears,
That ring with pain.

Brother, sister, I have a message for you.
Are ye a worker, are ye a farmer?
We are alike then.
Brother, sister,
We have no wrong when we are born;
We toil yet we have no bread;
We spin yet we have no shirt;
We do building yet we have no shed.

H.T. TSIANG

Awake, ye, brother,
Come hand in hand
To their defeat!
Brother, sister, there is a message for you:
Japan occupies Shantung,
But the toilers of Japan, they are with us;
Not Tanaka the oppressor,
Not Tanaka the murderer,
But the toilers of Japan will join us-
We together will crush Tanaka.

Brother, sister.
You are a farmer, you are a worker!
Hark to the cock,
A new day is coming!

Out of the ruthless mass-murder
March to Manchuria,
South of Canton;
Away with the exploiters-
When the sky with blood is red,
We all will have our bread!

May 24, 1928

H.T. TSIANG

Chinaman, Laundryman

"Chinaman"!
"Laundryman"!
Don't call me "man"!
I am worse than a slave.

Wash! wash!
Why can I wash away
The dirt of others' clothes
But not the hatred of my heart?
My skin is yellow,
Does my yellow skin color the clothes?
Why do you pay me less
For the same work?
Clever boss!
You know
How to scatter the seeds of hatred
Among your ignorant slaves.

Iron! iron!
Why can I smooth away
The wrinkles of others' dresses
But not the miseries of my heart?
Why should I come to America
To wash clothes?
Do you think "Chinamen" in China
Wear no dresses?
I came to America
Three days after my marriage.
When can I see her again?
Only the almighty "Dollar" knows!

Dry! dry!
Why do clothes dry,

But not my tears?
I work
Twelve hours a day,
He pays
Fifteen dollars a week.
My boss says,
"Chinaman,
Go back to China
If you don't feel satisfied!
There,
Unlimited hours of toil:
Two silver dollars a week,
If
You can find a job."
"Thank you, Boss!
For you remind me.
I know
Bosses are robbers
Everywhere!"

Chinese boss says:
"You Chinaman,
Me Chinaman
Come work for me—
Work for your fellow countryman!
By the way,
You 'Wong,' me 'Wong'—
Do we not belong to same family?
Ha! ha!
We are cousins!
Oh yes!
You 'Hai Shan,' me 'Hai Shan,'
Do we not come from same district?
O, come work for me;
I will treat you better!"
"GET away from here,
What is the difference,
When you come to exploit me?"

H.T. TSIANG

"Chinaman"!
"Laundryman"!
Don't call me "Chinaman"!
Yes, I am a "Laundryman"!
The workingman!
Don't call me "Chinaman"!
I am the Worldman
"The International Soviet
Shall be his human race"!

"Chinaman"!
"Laundryman"!
All the workingmen!
Here is the brush
Made of Marxism.
Here is the soap
made of Leninism.
Let us all
Wash with the blood!
Let us all
Press with the iron!
Wash!
Brush!
Dry!
Iron!
Then we shall have
A clean world.

August 15, 1928

H.T. TSIANG

Rickshaw Boy

What shall I do?
What shall I do?

Father, penniless! Rent? No.
He was a farmer, the year was bad, so
He killed himself a year ago.

Now soldiers come, the bugles blow,
Raping the women, you take them where you go!
O my mother, where do they keep you now?

Who can pay with father gone!
The landlord come, there is no one
Here but old, old folks with money gone!

The rich man smiles in garments of gold.
My elder sister but fifteen, must be sold.
The rich man cares for nothing—but women and gold.

Grandfather is too old to be a wage slave.
Grandmother stands near the edge of the grave.
No more firm-breasted sister of fifteen,
She is a concubine, though young and green.

What shall I do?
What shall I do?
Only one way:
I must leave today.

Faster than a horse can I move my legs,
Pulling the chaise I shall be a horse instead;
I shall not worry to earn my bread.

Ta! ta! ta! ta!
Pulling rickshaw!
How far, how far?
Way beyond the dimming star!

Ta! ta! ta! ta!
Pulling rickshaw!
How long, how long?
Till the moon has come and the sun has gone!

Ta! ta! ta! ta!
Pulling rickshaw!
The cruel wind ruffles my heavy hair!
The stormy rain washes my body in chilling air!

Ta! ta! ta! ta!
Pulling rickshaw!
On my back is my bed!
In the rickshaw is my shed!

Ta! ta! ta! ta!
Pulling rickshaw!
Surpassing the horse's speed!
Following the motor car in lead!

Ta! ta! ta! ta!
Pulling rickshaw!
My silent sobs are bitter, and I run and run!
The rich man smiles merrily, and has lots of fun!

Ta! ta! ta! ta!
Pulling rickshaw!
I beg for one copper tip,
The rich man answers with a ruthless kick!

Ta! ta! ta! ta!
Pulling rickshaw!
North! east! south! west!
Is the grave the only place a workingman may rest?

Ta! ta! ta! ta!
Pulling rickshaw!
International Park, no dogs nor "Chinese" admitted,
None but rich "Chinese" may be permitted!

Ta! ta! ta! ta!
Pulling rickshaw!
O, I shall die!
Blood pouring from this mouth of mine,
I shall die in the street's wet slime!
O missionary, you whip me with an extra dime,
Rushing to the station to meet your loving boy
    on time!

O! father, in death you are wasted low,
O! mother, who knows where you are now;
Sister, your misery is grandparents' woe.
Grandmother and father, you are not lonely in gloom,
For I still can feed you in my tomb.

O, horse, you are lucky! your master gives you care,
Sometimes he releases you in the fresh air,
O, motor car, you are lucky! Your master gives
    you care,
Sometimes he spends money for your repair.

O, rich man now you make me pull rickshaw,
Some day I will make you eat rickshaw!
O, fellow workingmen, only to you dare I cry!
How poor I die!
How poor I die!

O, workingman, you are rich men's fools!
Rich men use you for their tools!
O, workingmen, arise! Be no more fools!
O, workingmen, be nobody's tools!

September 1st, 1928

H.T. TSIANG

"He Was Satirizing"

...Try my pill—New Deal!
Hello,
Everybody:
How do you feel?"

When the deal was old,
We were told:
"Chicken in every pot!"
Now the deal is new—
So the guy is telling you.
I see no chicken hot.
And I even lost my little pot.

When the deal was old,
We were told:
"There is a little dark spot
In the sun, you see—
So the depression
Hits you and me."

But it's the same sun
In one country where
There's no depression—Why?
And the sun
Hurts no one!

When the deal was old,
We were told:
"Prosperity is right around the corner."
Now the deal is new—
So the guy is telling you.
I have bummed around
The corners of the West,

The corners of the East—
Dirt,
Starvation;
But where is prosperity
To be found?

When the deal was old,
We were told:
"Don't hurry!
Prosperity will be back right away."
Now the deal is new—
So the guy is telling you.
I have waited and waited.
How can I be in no hurry—
Since hunger knows no holiday?

When the deal was old
We were told:
"Everything takes time!"

But I haven't a nickel,
Not to say a dime.
How can I say "Dandy and fine!"
While in a breadline?

When the deal was old,
We were told:
"Hard times are here,
Because we have no beer."
Now the deal is new—
So the guy is telling you.
We now have beer,
But is prosperity here?

When the deal was old
We were told:
The garbage was full of filth.
But we could still have something

To pick up, and to chew,
In the wind of wintry cold.
Now the deal is new—
So the guy is telling you.
Rotten meat makes chopped meat.
When the chopped meat is rotten,
It makes sausage.
Nothing is left
In the garbage!
When the winter is over—
Here's the blessing of the Deal New:
Eating the morning dew!
Looking at the mountain-view!
Or singing the St. Louis Blues.

It's under this system!
It's under this system!

Mr. System
Beware:
The Hanging
On
Union Square!...

1935

BUNICHI KAGAWA

One Sun

Trees are standing

Never to lie down
To steal

A rest,

To rest their
Secret quiet.

One sun,
One song,
And one land:
My sandals burn

Absorbed

In the dreamy
Exposure of noon,

And I wander

Naively executing
My shadow-warm dream.

1930

BUNICHI KAGAWA

Hunger

The coal and glass and green leaves
Come from beneath the dark earth,
Crystallized, breathing, blazing,
In the flare of July sun.

Wonder at them; they will burn you whole
In your wonderment.
Speak to them; you shall be silenced
By their sharp secret.

Yet, here is a smell of sudden-civilization
In the smell of coal burning;
Here is a stark blow of soaring cubes compact
In glass and stone;
The sharp hunger of men shot into space,
And etched against the sheen of time,
Blazing-

1930

Silent Intimacy

The lovely ease of flowering
And fruiting of the trees,
Dreams through the old years,
That we may read therein
The civility of Nature's career.
Though in Nature there is no pity,
No answer and no memory,
One imperial afternoon is enough
To hold the remembered light
Of one years, now lost and dim.

1930

Hidden Flame

A portion of decayed smile magnified
Upon the mirror...
Or perhaps other belief or quietness
Nourished of its own leaves and ends
Now withers gradually within me
Like the noiseless death of light.

Life seen through the hollow caves
Of my eyes dotted with this or that
Of doubts or somehow or a belief
Crumbles like the wall of wind spent;
I touch it and the beyond with careful
Totality of my hand, the dense structure
Of a feel complete and mute.

And gradually, the dark flame of will
Lurking behind the hands that touch,
Hands that grasp, and hands that feel,
Eats into my body left mostly alone
Like the ceaseless pillar of waterfall.

1930

MOON KWAN

To Witter Bynner

I, a wanderer; thou a weaver of the petal-speech,
In the bridge-land of the East and West have met.
Though flowers may bloom and fall,
The Spring breeze shall not forget.

1932

Air Ride

Up! up in the air!
Drop! drop mortal care!
Here, here I am free
As winds would be!

Go! swift soaring car,
Challenge the shooting star!
I want to feel the soft bosom
Of yon white cloud
And tear away the gloomy sun's thick shroud!

What matter if I should fall?
As long as I hear freedom's call.
What can there be to fear
When heaven is so near!

1932

Coolie Song

Lay ah hown—
Off the traffic zone!

Lay ah hown—
Watch your own!

Lay ah hown—
Pull it alone!

Lay ah hown—
Watch the stone!

Lay ah hown—
Aching bone!

Lah ah hown—
The devil is known!

1932

ANONYMOUS

From *Island*

8

Instead of remaining a citizen of China, I willingly
    became an ox.
I intended to come to America to earn a living.
The Western styled buildings are lofty; but I have not
    the luck to live in them.
How was anyone to know that my dwelling place
    would be a prison?

8

國民不爲甘爲牛，

意至美洲作營謀。

洋樓高聳無緣住，

誰知棲所是監牢？

35

Leaving behind my writing brush and removing my
   sword, I came to America.
Who was to know two streams of tears would flow
   upon arriving here?
If there comes a day when I will have attained my
   ambition and become successful,
I will certainly behead the barbarians and spare not
   a single blade of grass.

35

留筆除劍到美洲，

誰知到此淚雙流？

倘若得志成功日，

定斬胡人草不留。

69

Detained in this wooden house for several tens of days,
It is all because of the Mexican exclusion law which
　　implicates me.
It's a pity heroes have no way of exercising their
　　prowess.
I can only await the word so that I can snap Zu's whip.

From now on, I am departing far from this building.
All of my fellow villagers are rejoicing with me.
Don't say that everything within is Western styled.
Even if it is built of jade, it has turned into a cage.

1910–1940

TOYO SUYEMOTO

Dusk

When dusk settles upon the heart
    As fog drifts inland from the bay
And slowly covers all the town
    At close of day,

Grayness will dim the vision then
    And night will make near things seem far—
But I shall look into the dark
    For some lost star.

1940

Attitude

I might have let the commonplace suffice:
Arisen at convenient hours each morn,
Dined simply at midday,
And then supped early with the dusk
And found dreamless sleeping in the night.
I might have let the small room close me in
With four blank walls and taken all
Contained within as mere necessities.
But two narrow windows have given me
Sufficient space to frame the sky
And a handful of stars.
I might have learned of unconcern,
But, oh, the urgencies the heart has known
Would never let me be,
And twilight conversation with the wind
Has taught me listening.

1941

The Dream

I have awakened from the dream:
  It is no more—
Now noghts to come will be
  As once before.

  Always a star will swing between
  The earth and sun,
But never nearer since
  The dream is done.

1941

Rationalized

Now distantly toward the west
  Through barriers of foreign air
And unpaved water, no one goes,
  No heart so rash to dare.

Who would be following the sun
  Beyond the depths of clouded seas?
Who would brave time to seek the lost
  And dim Hesperides?

For mind declares the apple no
  More golden, but stale bitter fruit
That was conceived in hostile earth
  Out of a cankered root.

1941

TOYO SUYEMOTO

In Topaz

Can this hard earth break wide
  The stiff stillness of snow
And yield me promise that
  This is not always so?

Surely, the warmth of sun
  Can pierce the earth ice-bound,
Until grass comes to life
  Outwitting barren ground!

1943

Hokku

The geese flew over
At dusk—I shivered, not with
Cold, but sense of loss.

Where do the geese go?
Can they escape from autumn
And return to spring?

Let me follow them:
The birds know better than I
Which way leads to spring.

1941

Retrospect

No other shall have heard,
  When these suns set,
The gentle guarded word
  You may forget.

No other shall have known
  How spring decays
Where hostile winds have blown,
  And that doubt stays.

But I remember yet
  Once heart was stirred
To song—until I let
  The sounds grow blurred.

And time—still fleet—delays
  While pulse and bone
Take count before the days
  Lock me in stone.

1945

HISAYE YAMAMOTO

Et Ego In America VIXI

My skin is sun-gold
My cheekbones are proud
My eyes slant darkly
And my hair is touched
With the dusky bloom of purple plums.
The soul of me is enrapt
To see the wisteria in blue-violet cluster,
The heart of me breathless
At the fragile beauty of an ageless vase.
But my heart flows over
My throat chokes in reverent wonder
At the unfurled glory of a flag—
    Red as the sun
    White as the almond blossom
    Blue as the clear summer sky.

1941

Spring Dirge

The first bud began to grow ere spring.
I waited to see unfold
These sharp-pointed tips, slow-transforming
From pale-green, waxed, perfect mold
Of Coldness and quiescent newness
To first glowing daffodil—
Yielding, swaying to the wind's caress,
Sunshine captured in bright yellow frill.
Then the saffron gold cup appearing,
Its promise of bright blossom
Sent my expectant heart loud singing.
Morning full flower would come.
I thought sun and glorious spring came
With that pure yellow bloom, when
Kneeling to smell of that sweet spring flame,
I found its heart worm-eaten.

1941

CHARLES YU

In America

The beat of a tom-tom
Breaks upon our senses
As we enter the vermilion door
Of the night club.
The air is a powder-blue shroud...
And from somewhere comes
The quickening scent of musk.
Seated, we order bacardi cocktails
And watch a beautiful Negress
Standing in a spot of ochre,
Her skin, brown as fresh iodine,
Her lips a coral lacquer.

Only in America could it occur:
This Negress passionately singing
Eli Eli Lomo Asovtoni,
The Yiddish lament
Written by a New Yorker
For a drama dealing
With Chinese Jews.

But studying her menu
Miss Jones observes:
You haven't seen anything yet.

1941

CHARLES YU

White Night in Chicago

The City has died
Into a white-hot breathlessness.
The room is filled
With a cloud-haze of smoke
And sound.
To my student friends
I am explaining
The structure of Chinese music
And they smile at the thought
Of only five notes
Without semitones.

We drink iced rice wine
And I play for them
Several recordings
Of the Shu-lute.

When these friends have left,
I will tear the sweat-drenched clothes
From my steaming back
And swing from the chandelier
In a loincloth.
One more rise of the thermometer
Will send me running thru the streets
Like a dog in fever.

Yet Miss Jones sits there
In her coolest manner
Eating lichee nuts
And talking of clothes
And the numerous men
Who admire her.

1941

JOSE GARCIA VILLA

57

I was not young long: I met the soul early:
Who took me to God at once: and, seeing
God the Incomparable Sight, I knelt my body

Humbly: whereupon God saw the star upon
My brow: stooped to kiss it: O then the
Blinding radiance there! explosion of all

My earthness: sparks flying till I was all
Embers: long, long did God hold me: till
He arose and bade me to rise saying : Now

Go back. Now go back from where you came.
Go back: Understanding is yours now. Only
Beware: *beware!* since you and God have lovered.

1942

Untitled ("When,I")

When,I,was,no,bigger,than,a,huge,
Star,in,my,self,I,began,to,write,
     My,
     Theology,
     Of,rose,and,

Tiger: till,I,burned,with,their,
Pure,and,Rage. Then,was,I,Wrath-
     Ful,
     And,most,
     Gentle: most,

Dark,and,yet,most,Lit: in,me,an,
Eye,there,grew: springing,Vision,
     Its,
     Gold,and,
     Its,wars. Then,

I,knew,the,Lord,was,not,my,Creator!
—Not,He,the,Unbegotten—but,I,saw,
     The,
     Creator,
     Was,I—and,

I,began,to,Die,and,I,began,to,Grow.

1962

DIANA CHANG

At the Window

So unnecessary, the whirling—
The white feathers whirling.
The puffed winter bird—
Need he take so slowly that bright inward look

This heart that cannot master it
Finds the snow unnecessary beauty.

1946

CARLOS BULOSAN

Factory Town

The factory whistle thrilled the atmosphere
With a challenging shriek; the doors opened suddenly
and vomited black-faced men, toil-worn men:
Their feet whispered wearily upon the gravel path;
They reached the gate and looked at each other.
No words—lidless eyes moved, reaching for love.
Silence and fear made them strong, invincible, wise.
They shook their hands and tossed their heads back
In secret defiance to their fragmentary careers,
And paced the homeward road with heavy hearts.

These were the longest years of their lives;
These were the years when the whistle at four o'clock
Drove them to the yard, then they scurried
Home heavy with fatigue and hunger and love.
These were the years when the gigantic chimneys blocked
The skies with black smokes that reminded passersby
Of a serpent-like whip of life within, bleeding,
Scarred with disease and death. These were the years...

Faces behind the laced doors and curtained windows,
Did you see the young man stand by the factory gate,
His face serious and forlorn, brittled with pain,
His hands unsteady with nervousness—did you see him?
Look at the lengthening line of voiceless men waiting
By the factory gate that will never be men again.

1935

CARLOS BULOSAN

Biography

There is no end of sadness
When winter came and sprawled over
The trees and houses, a man rose from
His sleep and kissed his wife who wept.
A child was born. Delicately the film
Of his life unfolded like a coral sea,
Where stone is hard substance of wind
And water leading into memory like pain.
He was a young man. He looked at himself
Through a glass that was too real to image
His face, unreal before his eyes. These were vivid
To the hands; these were too real
To the hearts that bled to sustain life.
He was a man. And the sun that leaped
Into his eyes, the grass beneath his feet
That walked cobbled streets, the cities-
All were a challenge to his imagination:
But his mother decaying in a nameless grave,
And his father watching a changing world
Through iron bars, his broken childhood,
Were as real as pain locking memory.

1937

CARLOS BULOSAN

If You Want To Know
What We Are

I.
If you want to know what we are who inhabit
forest, mountain, rivershore, who harness
beast, living steel, martial music (that classless
language of the heart), who celebrate labor,
wisdom of the mind, peace of the blood;

If you want to know what we are who become
animate at the rain's metallic ring, the stone's
accumulated strength, who tremble in the wind's
blossoming (that enervates earth's potentialities),
who stir just as flowers unfold to the sun;

If you want to know what we are who grow
powerful and deathless in countless counterparts,
each part pregnant with hope, each hope supreme,
each supremacy classless, each classlessness
nourished by unlimited splendor of comradeship;

We are multitudes the world over, millions everywhere;
in violent factories, sordid tenements, crowded cities,
in skies and seas and rivers, in lands everywhere;
our numbers increase as the wide world revolves
and increases arrogance, hunger, disease and death.

We are the men and women reading books, searching
in the pages of history for the lost word, the key
to the mystery of living peace, imperishable joy;
we are factory hands field hands mill hands everywhere,
molding, creating, building structures, forging ahead,

Reaching for the future, nourished in the heart;
we are doctors, scientists, chemists discovering,
eliminating disease and hunger and antagonisms;
we are soldiers, navy-men, citizens guarding
the imperishable will of man to live in grandeur.

We are the living dream of dead men everywhere,
the unquenchable truth that class-memories create
to stagger the infamous world with prophecies
of unlimited happiness-a deathless humanity;
we are the living and the dead men everywhere...

II.
If you want to know what we are, observe
the bloody club smashing heads, the bayonet
penetrating hollowed breasts, giving no mercy;
watch the bullet crashing upon armorless citizens;
look at the tear-gas choking the weakened lung.

If you want to know what we are, see the lynch
trees blossoming, the hysterical mob rioting;
remember the prisoner beaten by detectives to confess
a crime he did not commit because he was honest,
and who stood alone before a rabid jury of ten men.

And who was sentenced to hang by a judge
whose bourgeois arrogance betrayed the office
he claimed his own; name the marked man,
the violator of secrets; observe the banker,
the gangster, the mobster who kill and go free:

We are the sufferers who suffer for natural love
of man for man, who commemorate the humanities
of every man; we are the toilers who toil
to make the starved earth a place of abundance
who transform abundance into deathless fragrance.

We are the desires of anonymous men everywhere,
who impregnate the wide earth's lustrous wealth
with a gleaming fluorescence; we are the new thoughts
and the new foundations, the new verdure of the mind;
we are the new hope new joy life everywhere.

We are the vision and the star, the quietus of pain;
we are the terminals of inquisition, the hiatuses
of a new crusade; we are the subterranean subways
of suffering; we are the will of dignities;
we are the living testament of a flowering race.

If you want to know what we are—
WE ARE REVOLUTION!   1940

SOJIN TAKEI

Untitled

MP o matasete
nare ga totonoeshi
namoida komorishi
kaban no omoki

While the MP's wait
You fill my suitcase
And spill your tears.
How heavy its weight.

takazora wa
saku naki mama ni
yugarasu
izuchi hatenami
tobitsu kieyuku

1946

Untitled

There is no fence
High up in the sky.
The evening crows
Fly up and disappear
Into the endless horizon.

1946

IWAO KAWAKAMI

The Pebble

now here is a pebble—flat and flecked like a badly-
    painted Easter egg
(no plumb line touches yet the fronds in Tuscarora
    deep)
—how old is the moon, mother?
(I walked with Plato in a marble hall—Pythagoras and
    the triangle in the sand)
the boy rubs the pebble in a dirt-streaked palm
—may I have this dance, Adabelle?
(deepening dusk over a city—the frowning
    seismologist)
by the shores of Lake Tahoe there once stood an Indian
—and I am haunted by the music of your voice
(the mind broods over the hidden epicenter)
he listens to the Great Spirit speaking in the wind
—let no man asunder or forever hold his peace
(below the ocean ooze the earth is shifting)
through a cupped hand the boy sends an exultant
    shout to the green pines of the Sierras
—needles and pins, that's what babies are made of
(the upheaval beginning and water twisting toward the
    sky)
from the boy's hand the pebble describes a trajectory—
    eyes blinded by its invisible path across the sun
—the endless night—this primitive pain drawn
    through the wire of parturition
(the pebble sinks into the lake—the tidal wave
recedes—on the steps of the hospital the husband
    looks upon a new city)

1947

Transcontinental

and this eludes the reaching by the hand:
the strange intricacies of grass and sand,
of gray eagles in calculated flight,
of stars that turn on curtained gears at night,
of bare mountains sandpapered by the wind,
of plain-cropping cattle, thirsty and thinned,
of bleaching bones and invisible graves,
of dry heat dancing in sealess waves.

This is the land through which the express speeds
and Navajos fashion eternal beads.

1947

Iseult

I thought I heard the rising of the wind
This night, or did gods whisper when we kissed
And ponder if we have or have not sinned
In this, beloved one, our fear-torn tryst.
There is no world nor time within your eyes
And briefly darkness leaves a shadowed heart.
We watch the blue that spreads in morning skies—
That touches rims of love's remembered part.

So strange that in our summer we found spring,
Its fusing magic in our blood so late—
So late, you say, you cannot cry nor sing
In this unspoken hour. But wait—
    Was it the flicker of a lamp that swayed,
    Or did I see the shadow of a blade?

1947

Untitled

ikameshiki
nijyu no saku no
kanata niwa
murasaki niou
yama manekiori

Beyond the forbidding fence
Of double barbed wire,
The mountain, aglow in purple,
Sends us its greetings

1957

Untitled

junjitsu no
uchi ni ryoyu
mitari yukinu
kono tatkai no
hate o mizushite

Within just ten days
Three fellow internees
Depart from this world
Never to see
The end of this war.

1957

From *Sounds from the Unknown*

KANSHU OKUTARA

Taiyo wa
sora yori aoi
kono tabi wa
oya wo tozunete
teimai ga noru.

This time as my younger brother and sister
Take ship to visit our parents,
> The color
> Of the ocean
> Is bluer than the sky.

SHIGEO KIKUCHI

Hateshi naku
shio uchiyosuru
ganto ni
umi no rekishi no
sozoro tachikuru.

As I stood
On top of the cliff,
Watching the endless tide come in,
I slowly became aware
That the history of the ocean
Lay before me.

SHINOBU YAMASHIRO

Aisareshi
kioku bakari ga
kagirinashi
tosarishi kimi yo
soto te wo awasu.

My sweetheart
Now gone so far away—
    In remembrance
    Of our limitless love,
    I secretly clasp my hand.

KIYOKO SAKAKURA

Hita gokoro
inori tsuzukete
ware wa tatsu
sokan chomon no
imin kwan no mae.

Standing in front
Of the officer
At the immigration hearing,
With all my heart wishing to remain here,
I steadily continued my prayers.

KIYOKO WATANABE

Fukeshi yo no
yuami no shijima
mado no to no
basho wo uchite
hisme suguru oto.

While taking mybath,
In the deep silent night,
The banana leaves,
Drenched with icy rain,
Beat against the window.

KOSHU HATANAKA

Ikurucho
igi ni kodawari
utsusu me ni
mado no hachiue no
hi ni katamukite tatsu.

Thinking about the meaning
Of having life,
My eye was drawn out of the window
To the potted plants
Bowing their heads to the sun.

MAYUMI KUMAGAI

Furusato e
okuru tsutsumi ni
kuwaetaki
shina amata ari
kure no tento.

At the end of the year
There are so many things
In the store windows
That I want to add to the package
Going to my homeland.

(Translation: Lucille M. Nixon and Tomoe Tann)

1963

FRED WAH

They are Burning

Pitch black up the valley
in front of us twenty miles
they are burning the mountains down
the sky is that kind of orange
the hillsides are outlined to us
in just that orange horizon
which will be gone with daybreak
when the smoke of their burning
hangs ove rthe valleys rivers and trees
drifts slowly on the contours of the land
and the deadness where no birds fly.

Yes they are burning
for it is July
and August and the nights
with no wind the darkness is cool.

What I thought would be there is not
I'm sorry to say. What I had expected
was to sleep for the ride with eyes closed
not drive into a burning mountainside.

1965

FRED WAH

Mountain

Mountain come over me in my youth
     green grey orange of colored dreams
   darkest hours of no distance
       Mountain full of creeks ravines of rock
  and pasture meadow snow white ridges humps of granite
    ice springs trails twigs stumps sticks leaves moss
      shit of bear deer balls rabbit shit
   shifts and cracks of glaciation mineral
O Mountain hung over me in these years of fiery desire
    burns on your sides your many crotches rocked
       and treed in silence from the winds
  Mountain many voices nameless curves and pocked in shadows
         not wild but smooth
   your instant flats flat walls of rock
      your troughs of shale and bits
soft summer glacier snow
     the melting edge of rounded stone
  and cutting of your height the clouds
   a jagged blue
        your nights your nights alone
  your winds your winds your grass
     your lying slopes your holes your traps
   quick blurs of all my dreams
Mountain poem of life
  true and real
    reeling Mountain burning mind
  stand word stand letter
    voice in whisper secret repeating cries
  stand in rock stretch out
   in all ways to the timber line
  spread over all valleys run cool the waters down
    from luminous white snows
      your cracks

O creek song flow always an utter pure of coolness
      spring from the rocks
sing in the hot thirsty my sticky tongue
          my jaw catch below the bridge
Yes my jaw for your waters hangs
    catch of water soothe the sweat
      sweet cold on teeth in flow and eddy
in swirl my gut it fills and bloats with fluid mountain

1967

SUNITI NAMJOSHI

Pinocchio

And if I spoke to you, what would I say?
That there's a change? That I can still feel the ground
Shifting and giving under my feet?
That you are made of ivory and steel
And very beautiful, and I'm afraid
To smudge the miracle with my fingertips?
I'm content to look in the moonlight,
To parody my own wonder, to wear
A powdered mask—how white the mask in the
        moonlight—
And turn cartwheels about you. Oh be a ghost
In the moonlight, be a dream. That you should be real
Terrifies me. Don't move. Don't speak.
If you speak let your words be contained in the veil.
My face is a mask in the moonlight. I'm a doll
made of brown wood. My features never change.
If you are a doll carved in ivory,
We may—it is permitted—dance
A minuet in the moonlight. But don't,
I beg you, don't slip. If we should stumble
And clutching one another, discover
We're neither wood nor ivory, they'd switch on
The lights and the children would scream
And we would have to move
To the other side of the curtain.

1966–67

Jacob-for Wes

I want to know a man of war
I want to know a man who
Wars because he is the centre
Wars within his centre against
His centre. A man who destroys
His centre. A man who is
No centre. I want to know the
Touch of a man who knows
My war. I want to know a
Man destroyed by love.

1967

JOY KOGAWA

Righteous Cleansing

Here we are
Washing our hands
Cleansing of all dirt
All skin
All blood, nerve, sinew,
All bone,
Making transparent
Our clean clean
Clean hands

1967

JESSICA TARAHATA HAGEDORN

Filmore Street Poems: August 1967

1.

Into the deepest mornings
Strange harmonious cries are sung
By roving leopards
Who shatter windows   and minds
Exalting the cunts
Of fresh young girls

2.

Sweet soft face
Bloated and defiled
By morticians and priests:
There are violent celebrations
In the street

3.

The Chinaman knows it all
Keeps secrets locked up
Inside a vintage cash register

4.

At the corner
One glimpses
Occasional dreams
Hung-out to dry by twenty-five-year-old women
Whose backs are stooped.
They have looked away
From me before
And will again (having understood what I wasted)

5.

GOLDSTEIN'S-GOLDFARB'S-WE BUY AND SELL
Blond wigs and
Hard round asses   strutting
Before the dull gold eyes of men
Waiting to call out truth
To strangers
                BUT

6.

The Chinaman has truth
Locked up
In his cash register too

7.

Gunfire spit
In the distance
The young fresh girls
Have left the street
The construction zone
Will resound tomorrow
It doesn't make a difference
Who died yesterday

They have looked away
From us before
But not again.

1967

A Script: Beauty is the beginning of terror...

1. The sea.
2. The disappearance of the sun.
3. My love is red like blood.
4. The Sky.
5. My eye.
6. That monster, sleep, is hungry.
7. Young girls' faces.
8. White statues.
9. My love is red like blood.
10. Or I would die, the black revolver embracing me.

1968

G.S. SHARAT CHANDRA

Bharata Natyam Dancer

jana jan jana jan was the sound of the dancer's feet
dana dan dana dan was the sound of the accompanying drum
and the occasion was the inauguration of the new city hall
and the dancer was the daughter of the famous court dancer
who was too well known to be named

and the people applauded
because the ministers applauded

was she a dancer
or the cousin of an elephant
no one dared to wonder
for she was the daughter of her famous mother
who was decorated by many rajas and noblemen
who had gone to america as cultural representative of the country
who was a great social hostess
who had many friends and relatives in the government

great dancer, said the journalists
that's why we invited her, said the mayor
we always had her mother here, said the entertainment committee
should be sent to europe as cultural delegate, said the deputy
        minister for culture
yes, said the minister for finance
i knew her mother. . .said the chief minister,
and people watched the ministers the mayor
and the entertainment committee
and nodded their heads in approval
when the ministers the mayor and the entertainment committee
nodded their heads
and it was one big nodding of heads
wearing the white cap of the congress party   1968

MAY WONG

Spring Comes to Kresge Co.

Why lilies for Easter?
Why rabbits? Why Spring?

The rabbits are horrible.
They stuffed the air.

They left their glass eyes
in your head. A blue rabbit,

A pink rabbit, a bald rabbit,
they multiply like mad.

This one has a soft expression.
It has no heir.

It will soon infest the rest.
The rabbits are terrible.

They are all chewing gum.
There's a pantie,

A pantie for all sizes.
A bra, a bra for all

sizes. A wash-and-wear
woman, serving coffee,

She sells her hair.
There's a manager

His oval head shines like
a 60-watt bulb.

MAY WONG

There're some fish
at the back, they

carry themselves
in plastic bags. The eggs

are all in chocolate,
they will not make a mess.

The lilies are for Easter.
The lilies are made of quick-

silver. The hyacinths are sweet,
they are not for believers.

The tulips so cheap this year
they look like wax. This year,

nothing is greener
than the cut-throat lotion

this year, green like some
secrets. Bending over

the birthday cards (like
a camel on 3 legs) the old lady

asks me to pick her one
her mouth is chicken-blood fresh

1969

Bastard

The sun is hatching itself
The sun is hatching itself
The sun

has been hatching itself
for God knows

how many years
the sun has been

We will not live to see it
We will not live

The sun is hatching itself

1969

M. LAKSHMI GILL

Rain

Ink flows down the sky
black rain, like water
dripping on a fresh-
written page

black rain, washing away
the words, the verbs of our
life unheeding the frantic
rush to save

1970

LAWSON INADA

West Side Songs

I. Whiterarama

Catch the skyline, baby—
Security, Towne House,
P. G. & E.

Know what I mean?
That's Whitearama, baby,
the big wide screen.

II. Something Holds

Somethings holds
it in place.
Something keeps it
from exploding.
Otherwise, it would be
all wars rolled
into one—Mexicans
punctured on chopsticks,

Blacks gagging
on crucifixes, curses
croaking in broken
English . . .

But wait . . .

That's why the railroad
snakes through
the town like a fence.

That's why they
toss in a few
wigs and grey suits

and sit, and wait.

III. Purple

Purple
the grape.
Purple
the mind
aged
in wine.
Purple
the vine
wine
cannot
puncture.
Purple
the face
burning
on trays
of new
empty
lots of
purple
Urban Renewal.

IV. "Sunset"

The sun never sets
on the Mexican
section—"Sunset."
Big street lights
keep them awake,

out of trouble,
fingering the hoes
of Mexican golf.
Mexicans commute
to find trouble.
They sing. They cut.
At wrestling arenas,
Mexicans beat
the bad Japanese.
Mexicans are fun.

The sun never sets
on the Mexican
section. It never comes up.

V. "Jericho"

"Jericho's"
a citadel,
slab of plaster
by the Black villas
by the slaughterhouse
by the city dump.

Policedogs keep
vigil—
sniffing out
White men, a minstrel cop.

Upstairs, slabs
on the racks.
You can stab them
and giggle.

You can get in
and wiggle.

Downstairs, the dice's
mammy grin.
The juke box
squeals the blues—
drunk
on a funky
harmonica.

Blackies stay happy.

Mornings, when Black
garbagemen come,
they play
buckets
like drums.

Sometimes, a Black
foetus dances
out in the gutter,
with ribs.

Come on over
and wail—

"Jericho", slaughterhouse,
dump.

VI. Okies

I always thought an Okie
was a white man gone fake—
play-acting, a spy.

Now I know Okies
are okay.
The dig music.
They cut each other up.

LAWSON INADA

VII. Armenians

are screwed up.
I mean
they won't move
to the West Side.
They're known
as the Fresno Jews.

They're screwed up.
I mean
they shave
names and noses
and herd hairy
Mustangs to school.

VIII. He-Ro

You know
about the sound
barrier.
Well don't you know
Willie broke
the color
barrier screaming
through White town
with a White girl
at 95 per.

After
the funeral,
his Cadillac
hub-caps flew
over in formation,
in tribute.

IX. Filipinos

are sharp.
They's why
they're barbers.
Sharp
trousers,
sharp
elevator shoes.
When they see
White girls
they go
"Sook sook sook sook."

X. Chinks

Ching Chong Chinaman
sitting on a fence
trying to make a dollar
chop-chop all day.

"Eju-kei-shung! Eju-kei-shung!"
that's what they say.

When the War came,
they said, "We Chinese!"
When we went away,
they made sukiyaki,
saying, "Yellow all same."

When the war closed,
they stoned the Japs' homes.

Grandma would say:
"Marry a Mexican,
a Nigger, just don't
marry no Chinese."

XI. Japs

are great
imitators—
they stole
the Greeks'
skewers,
used them
on themselves.
Their sutras
are Face
and Hide.
They hate
everyone else,
on the sly.

They play
Dr. Charley's
games—bowling,
raking,
growing forks
on lapels.
Their tongues
are yellow
with "r's",
with "l's."

They hate
themselves,
on the sly. I
used to be
Japanese

1970

YUKI HARTMAN

Untitled

A concrete lip, a visibly
Clean skull had the veins
Pooled up blood and clay
Sealed down the water vines

To dip the lip with early
Songs that sang the utter
New things to the body:
Concrete lip, opened there.

1970

BIOGRAPHICAL NOTES

Carlos Bulosan is best known for his novel *America is in the Heart*. Bulosan helped found the United Cannery and Packing House Workers of America and worked as a union organizer and writer. His writings also include *Dark People* and *Letters from America*.

G.S. Sharat Chandra is the author of numerous books, including *Aliens, April in Nanjagud, Bharat Natyam Dancer, The Ghost of Meaning, Heirloom, Offsprings of Servagna, Once or Twice*, and *Will This Forest*.

Diana Chang was an undergraduate at Barnard College when *Poetry* published three of her poems, including "At the Window." She did not realize then that she would continue to write and publish poetry, and become the author of six novels. She has been an editor in book publishing, and is also a painter who has exhibited in solo and group shows. She is the recipient of a John Hay Whitney Opportunity Fellowship that made it possible for her to start writing her first novel, *The Frontiers of Love*, originally published by Random House and recently reissued by the University of Washington Press. Her other awards include a Fulbright Scholarship, Mademoiselle Magazine Woman-of-the-Year Award and a grant from the New York State Council on the Arts.

Jun Fujita is the author of *Tanka: Poems in Exile*.

Lakshmi Gill is the author of *During Rain, I Plant Crysanthemums, First Clearing, Mind Walls*, and *Novena to St. Jude Thaddeus*.

Jessica Tarahata Hagedorn was born and raised in the Philippines. She is a well-known performance artist, poet, and playwright. She is the author of *Dangerous Music, Pet Food* and *Tropical Apparitions*, and *Danger and Beauty*. Her first novel, Dogeaters, appeared in 1990 and was nominated for the National Book Award.

Masao Handa is the author of *I Am a Firefly and Other Poems*.

Sadakichi Hartman was born in 1867 on an island in Nagasaki Harbor. He was educated in Germany. He is the author of *Drifting Flowers of the Sea and Other Poems to Elizabeth Blanche Walsh, Japanese Rhythms, Haik{ai} and Other Forms Translated, Adapted, or Imitated by Sadakichi Hartman, My Rubaiyat, Naked Ghosts: Four Poems*, and *Tanka and Haiku: 14 Japanese Rhythms*.

Yuki Hartman was born in Tokyo, Japan and currently lives in New York. He is the author of *A One of Me, Hot Footsteps, Red Rice* and *Ping*.

Lawson (Fusao) Inada is the author of *Before the War: Poems as They Happened*. He is an editor of two Asian American anthologies, *Aiiieeeee!* and *The Big Aiiieeeee!* With Garrett Hongo and Alan Chong Lau, he wrote *The Buddha Bandits Down Highway 99* (Buddhahead Press, 1978). He is a Professor of English at Southern Oregon State College. He and his wife, Janet, have two sons, Miles and Lowell.

Bunichi Kagawa is the author of *Hidden Flame*.

Iwao Kawakami is the author of *The Parents and Other Poems* and and the first editor of Pacific Citizen.

Joy Kogawa was born in Vancouver, British Colombia in 1935. She is author of *Woman in the Woods* (Mosaic Books, 1985) *Road* (McClelland & Stewart, 1977), and *The Splintered Moon* (University New Brunswick, 1967). Her novels include *Obasan* (Lester& Orpen Dennys, 1981, Anchor 1994), and *Itsuka* (Viking Canada 1992). She has also written a book of children's fiction, Naomi's Road (Oxford University Press, 1986.

Moon Kwan is the author of *A Chinese Mirror*.

Suniti Namjoshi has taught in the department of English at the University of Toronto and now lives and writes in Devon, England. She has published numerous poems, fables, articles, and reviews in anthologies, collections and journals in India, Canada, the U.S., Australia, and Britain. Her latest work, *Saint Suniti and the Dragon* and a new edition of *Feminist Fables* have been published by Spinifex Press (1993) and Virago Press (1994)

Yone Noguchi was born in Japan in 1875. He is the

author of *From the Eastern Shore, The Ganges Call Me, Japanese Hokkus, Noguchi's Song Unto Brother Americans, The Pilgrimage, Seen and Unseen, The Selected Poems of Yone Noguchi, The Summer Cloud, These Scattered Flowers of My Poetry,* and *The Voice of the Valley.* He returned to Japan in 1904 and became a professor of English at Keio University.

Keiho Soga's poems featured in *Poets Behind Barbed Wire,* ed./trans. Nakano and Nakano, were selected from his tanka anthology *Keiho Kashm* (1957).

Toyo Suyemoto has published numerous poems.

Sojin Takei's poems featured in *Poets Behind Barbed Wire,* ed./trans. Nakano and Nakano, were selected from his wartime tanka anthology *Arena* (1946).

H.T. Tsiang has published *Poems of the Chinese Revolution, China Red, The Hanging on Union Square,* and *And China Has Hands.* Alan Wald describes him as "among the most innovative and idiosyncratic writers drawn to the United States Communist cultural movement of the Great Depression."

Jose Garcia Villa is from the Philippines. He was educated in New Mexico and New York. He has edited many magazines, and has a long list of writings, including *Footnote to Youth* (1933), *Many Voices* (1939), *Poems* (1941), *Volume II* (1949), *Selected Stories* (1962), and *The Essential Villa* (1965). He currently lives in New York.

Wen I-to's poem was anthologized in *Twentieth Century Chinese Poetry,* ed. Kai-yu Hsu.

Fred Wah is a teacher of Creative Writing and Poetics at the University of Calgary. He has published 16 books of poetry since 1965. More recent volumes include *Alley Alley Home Free* (Red Deer College Press, 1992), *So Far* (Talon Books, 1991), *Breathing My Name with a Sigh* (Talonbooks, 1981), and *Loki is Buried at Smokey Creek: Selected Poems* (Talon Books, 1980).

Wong May is the author of *A Bad Girl's Book of Animals, Reports,* and *Superstitions.*

Hisaye Yamamoto was born in California in 1921. Her short stories have been widely published in such magazines and journals as *Partisan Review, Kenyon Review, Furioso,*

Arizona Quarterly, and have also appeared in *Asian American Authors* (1972), *Asian American Heritage* (1974), *Aiiieeee: An Anthology of Asian American Writers* (1975), and *Counterpoint* (1976). Her collection of short stories *Seventeen Syllables and Other Stories* was published by Kitchen Table: Women of Color Press in 1988.

Charles Yu is the author of *Poems of a Chinese Student*.

Reminiscences: Asian North American Poetry Scenes (ca 1970 to mid-1980s)

COMPILED BY WALTER K. LEW

LOOKING BACK: BASEMENT WORKSHOP, 1971-86

FAY CHIANG, NEW YORK (1986)

In the fall of 1971, I got a call to come to a meeting of artists and writers at a place called Basement Workshop working on an art project called "Yellow Pearl." Located in the cellar of a tenement at 54 Elizabeth Street in New York Chinatown, Basement's two rooms had faulty plumbing which sometimes created small tidal pools on the concrete floor; at such times, the volunteer staff would ease the water towards the drain with a broom. I was shown an orange crate and a four-drawer filing cabinet and informed that this was The Asian American Resource Center, "the only collection of its kind on the east coast." People were sitting on brown boxes, which turned out to be packed with issues of Bridge magazine. An old door found on the street served as a table when placed atop crates.

At this particular meeting , I walked into a very intense argument and discussion. I had never seen so many (about 30) Asian American artists, writers, and musicians crammed together for a four-hour meeting. They were sipping cold duck, which they kept chilled by placing it in the water of the toilet tank. A fine arts major at the time, my assignment was to illustrate a few poems and prose pieces for the magazine. Tentatively, I offered the fact that I wrote poetry. "Bring it in," I was told. Later I was very excited to find out that my poems would be published and that someone was assigned to illustrate them.

So began a year-long project to raise money to produce "Yellow Pearl". I remember a benefit dance we held at Earl Hall at Columbia University; a lot of people came up from Chinatown, and we collected the gang kids' guns and put them away in a brown paper bag for safe keeping while they danced. We raised three thousand dollars that year, and "Yellow Pearl" was published in spring of '72.

As I spent more time at Basement, I gradually learned about its beginning. Founded in 1970–71 by Danny N.T. Yung and a group of fellow urban planners at Columbia University, professional writers Frank Ching and Margaret Loke, and people like Peter Pan and Eleanor Yung, it was an outgrowth of the research and data compiled for the Chinatown Report 1969 funded by the Ford Foundation. After the study was completed, Danny and his colleagues wanted to continue compiling information about Asian American communities—the germ for the Asian American Resource Center. Another idea Frank Chin supported was a journal publication, subsequently named *Bridge*.

This group of artists, writers, and musicians first gathered during the summer at the time of the Summer Health Fair which took place on Mott Street. Organizers raised the issue of health care for the community and the setting up of a Health Clinic staffed by volunteer health professionals. Musicians Charlie Chin, Nobuko Miyamoto, and Chris Iijima wrote and performed songs about Asian American identity, politics, and history. After the Health Fair, those involved decided to put the music into print, illustrate it, and add more poetry and prose.

Like myself, many of the people at Basement were second-generation Chinese Americans who had lived most of their lives in the boroughs of the city, and whose parents worked in laundries, sweatshops, shirt-press factories, or restaurants. As our parents toiled away, we were expected to graduate from Ivy League schools, marry and raise families, and quest earnestly for the promises of the

American Dream—not to become artists, writers, musicians, dancers, choreographers, activists, and community organizers.

Others were third-generation Japanese Americans, who had witnessed the scars from the internment camps during World War Two on their parents and grandparents. Still others were foreign-born, from Hong Kong, who had come to New York to pursue their education, remained for professional reasons, and settled with their families. Then there were those who had grown up and lived all their lives in the narrow streets of Chinatown, a predominantly immigrant community whose second generation was just entering the universities, or not.

Prior to the fall of 1971, many of our paths had already crossed. Some of us were involved in the Anti-War movement, organizing demonstrations, panel discussions, leafletting, and working with larger coalitions. We were also involved in campus organizing for Asian American, ethnic, women's, and gay studies programs. By organizing the Asian American students on campus—via clubs and student organizations—we were able to become more visible and make the needs of these students known. We were able to increase financial aid and student club budgets, and gain university support for Asian American studies courses, counseling, and professional referral services.

Wrestling with the question of Asian American identity and a place in this society, forced many of us to question what was happening with this country domestically and with its policies abroad. Following the history of American discrimination against its peoples of color, racist legislation on immigration, employment, housing, marriage, and ownership of property, the Civil Rights movement, Free Speech movement, Anti-War movement, and watching our inner cities burn in rage and frustration as our people, our dreams were shot down one by one with our leaders— Malcolm X, the Kennedys, Martin Luther King—many of our generation could not sit still. We had to act.

We also took heart and looked for models from the people struggling for liberation and survival in Vietnam, China, and the emerging nations in Africa.

Many of us traveled west visiting Asian American communities in San Francisco and Los Angeles. There we met peers who were also organizing and doing political, cultural, and social work. This was the beginnings of the Asian American movement. We were inspired by the working models of such organizations as Yellow Brotherhood (a drug rehabilitation center for youth), *Gidra* newspaper, Visual Communications (media), East West Players (theater and dance), and several of the Asian American studies departments in the University of California system. In San Francisco, there were the Kearny Street Workshop (a writers' collective), the Asian American Theater Workshop, and Japanese American Media Workshop.

Back in the Basement in New York, I was not alone. There was an entire group of people asking very similar questions, willing to work very hard on a volunteer basis to get art projects off the ground, organize around community issues of education, employment, housing, health, and mental health. These were exciting times.

Growing up in the back room of a laundry in Queens had proved isolating. I was caught between a world created at home by immigrant parents with values of the old world and the one outside made of school and friends. Fitting in neither world, those like myself would begin to build a new one.

· · · · · ·

Following the successful publication of "Yellow Pearl" we received a small seed grant from the National Endowment for the Arts, of which I became the coordinator. In January of 1973, the program was named Amerasia Creative Arts. With a core of twelve Asian American artists and art students, we designed a series of workshops in silkscreening, photography, dance, music and creative writing. That summer we also applied for support for thirty Neighborhood Youth Corps summer internships and ran workshops for youth from the community. We ran an Afterschool Arts and Crafts program for children from kindergarten through the sixth grade.

Three nights before a New York State Council on the Arts deadline, I was asked by the director to write up a proposal for the organization. With little experience, I plunged in. Luckily, by then I had met Carolyn Curran who had begun Seven Loaves, a coalition of arts and other organizations on the Lower East Side that provided training in fundraising and management. Basement became a founding member, along with Charas, The Lower East Side Printshop, Cityarts Workshop, The Children's Art Workshop, El Teatro Ambulante, and the Fourth Street "i," among others. Serving as a panelist on the Expansion Arts program gave me an overview of the many organizations doing community arts nation-wide. Here was another meaning to the word "community."

Through Seven Loaves, Basement met foundation and corporate funders; and as the quality of our programs increased, we received greater levels of funding. During the first year, I single-handedly raised $154,000 as a volunteer. The organization was governed by an unwieldy collective called the Executive Board, which moved along month by month with a great deal of yelling. Trying to pass on administrative and managerial information I learned from Seven Loaves to members of the Board, I was called to task a few years later by some of my peers as an "organizational misleader and a sellout to the people in the face of federal and state funding."

My first dealings with NYSCA was with Frank Diaz, who to my amazement pulled out Basement's files and flung them to my feet across the floor. He demanded I explain to him what it all meant. I asked him to read through the material. In hindsight, what may have confused Frank was the multi-disciplinary nature of the organization. At the time the concept of multi-disciplinary activities had not circulated widely.

While supporting the overhead of four locations (three loftspaces and a storefront), we continued to publish *Bridge* and run the Amerasia Creative Arts program and Asian American Resource Center. Through our Community

Planning Workshop Program, we also ran weekly Survival English and Citizenship classes for 200 community adults, as well as an after-school Arts and Crafts program for forty children and 160 Neighborhood Youth Corps interns each summer, with a staff of twelve youth workers administrating the program. From the west coast there came a steady stream of artist and community friends, some who literally camped out at Basement. Through talks and slide shows, both coasts kept in touch. Within Amerasia Creative Arts, a core of artists had begun working collectively on projects, programs and workshops. Sharing and teaching each other art skills, we wanted to create an art and a culture reflective of our experiences and political sensibilities. Some of us were also involved in Seven Loaves and Cityarts Workshop. We contributed to community issues by providing publicity materials, graphics and posters. One eventful night, we screened 2,000 posters for a community-wide demonstration against police brutality at City Hall. Basement had also received a National Endowment for the Humanities grant to do oral histories of senior citizens, and establish an old photograph collection, projects begun by Danny Yung and Fay Chew.

During 1974-75 there was a deep political schism within the organization. One of the two camps was for community arts and resources; the other was for partisan political organizing. Friends, families and former co-workers were split and the organization was on the verge of exploding.

In June 1975, I attended a meeting where a position paper drafted by the members of the partisan group was read accusing me of selling out the community to the federal and state government by accepting arts funding. I had become the victim of an organizational purge. At the end of the meeting I was literally pinned to the floor as I tried to protest. The body of 75 people left in hysteria. For several months I was harassed and followed about on the streets of Chinatown, as this group tried to "break" me.

In August 1975, I formalized a compromise, and implemented a gradual—though sickeningly disheartening—

separation of the arts and resources from partisan politics. Centralizing, we gave up two loft sites and a storefront (being much in arrears with rent, we paid up and left). We maintained the 22 Catherine Street loft and signed a four-year lease outside of Chinatown at 199 Lafayette.

To our detractors, Basement was leaving the community. We were. Given the political climate of the left and right within the community (the new forces challenging the traditional leadership of the old), the community became an arena of contracted death threats, beatings, and violence. Mildly put, it was confusing. I did not want to be caught in the crossfire. Having chaired a community meeting between the left and right earlier in the spring, I realized neither group was speaking to issues dealing with the real needs of this community and its people, but rather the demands and righteousness of each political party's beliefs.

At 199 Lafayette, there were 8,000 square feet of raw space and a single light bulb dangling from the ceiling. With a handful of people who shared a similar vision of creating an Asian American culture, we rolled up our sleeves and dug in. We put in plumbing, electrical lines, sheetrocked walls, and painted, all the while maintaining our daily administrative and programmatic activities.

My typical day during this period (1975-'76) began with an early morning commute from Queens of an hour and a half. Once at the office, I put in supply orders for lumber or whatever building materials were needed for the day and night's construction work. A meeting of staff began at 10:30 a.m. followed by more meetings, paperwork, telephone calls, and still more meetings until 6 in the evening. Then it was construction work with volunteers until midnight. With co-worker Patsy Ong and support from Pauline Eng and Meeling Wong, we kept it up for a year.

Within a year we had built a professional darkroom, an eight-track sound studio, administrative offices, a resource collection and library, a graphic design studio, silkscreen facilities, a wood workshop and a multi-purpose dance, rehearsal and performance space. Given the facilities, artists who had no previous links to the Chinatown community, but were from other parts of the country gravitated to Basement bringing their skills and resources.

Jack Tchen, historian from Chicago, coordinated the Asian American Resource Center with educator Gin Woo from Seattle; John Woo (also from Seattle), painter and graphic artist, developed the silkscreen program and facilities, and a design studio for the organization. Writers Richard Oyama, Teru Kanazawa, Jason Hwang, Susan Yung, and Helen Wong edited an anthology *American Born and Foreign* (Sunbury Press), and created a visibility for Asian American writers and musicians in the city through non-stop readings. CETA choreographer Theodora Yoshikami worked with other dancers and choreographers in presenting classes and concerts. Christian Frey, professional photographer, built a darkroom from scratch, while soundman Mike Friese created an eight-track sound studio with the assistance of Victor Huey and Geoff Lee.

While performing in the lead role in Broadway's "Pacific Overtures," Mako taught an acting workshop on Mondays, inspiring a body of individuals to commit their lives to the arduous task of becoming professional actors. Musicians Charlie Chin, Geoff Lee, and Kuni Mikami drew a range of musicians to perform and jam together.

At 22 Catherine, we still ran the children's programs (led by Don Kao) and the youth program (led by Pauline Eng, then Charlie Lai), the kids participating in many arts workshops. Throughout this period, there was tension between community and non-community people as to whose organization it was.

However, we made great leaps in the programming. Connections with artists and arts service organizations in the other minority, ethnic, alternative, and experimental spaces broadened our audience, and created greater visibility for Asian American artists in New York and nationwide. I believe this helped to increase funding for Asian American artists, also resulting in fellowships, grants, residences, and an increase of funding for Asian American cultural groups.

Exhausted, I took a leave of absence in 1977. During my time away, the staff I had developed decided they could do a better job if they forced me out. By April 1979, however, I was approached to return to the organization as a fundraiser. Board members resigned, staff departed, the organization was over $25,000 in debt, the bookkeeper went to Florida (with the books), the IRS was banging on the doors, former employees were screaming for back pay, and the creditors were threatening court suits. Morale was horrible.

We lost our lease at 199 Lafayette and were forced to move back to the much smaller space at 22 Catherine. During this period I weighed the pros and cons of trying again. I thought, we fail when we don't learn from our mistakes. Back in the city I got a job as a waitress to support myself (the late shift from five to midnight) so that during the day I could do organizational work. We had to begin again.

Three volunteers and I spent the better part of the year cleaning and sorting, getting an audit done. By then, we had located our bookkeeper who sent back our books. (It turned out that the IRS, which had threated to put us in jail for non-payment of taxes, owed Basement $134.) Next, we donated our darkroom, silkscreen, and other resources to other non-profit organizations; the Asian American Resource Center, for instance, went to the Chinatown History Project.

The focus from 1981 onward was to support the work of emerging and professional artists. Our strongest program to date has been the literature program coordinated by Jessica Hagedorn and myself. This I attribute to our association with the larger literary community and the heartening support we find from other writers and writer organizations.

The Morita Dance Company has produced dance concerts and Interarts performances under the directorship of choreographer Theodora Yoshikami. Jessica Hagedorn was instrumental in developing the Performance Poetry Workshop with Laurie Carlos.

In 1982, we began a series of Folk Arts Workshops. Often our emerging artists were frustrated by "not making it." We tuned to our older folk artists to learn how they had integrated life with art in a lifelong working process. I was looking for a useful approach and sense of meaning to one's life within the context of this larger society, the forces of which tended to reduce them to insignificance.

Also in 1985, we began a Play Reading Series under the directorship of Ernest Abuba with the assistance of Mary Lum. Working with a playwright and with script in hand, actors improvised on the material; suggestions from which the playwright would take under consideration in rewriting. The play was then presented in a reading to the public, followed by a discussion with director, playwright, and actors.

Don Kao and Linda Lew coordinated the Center for Educational Equity under Basement's umbrella. Working with junior high, high school and college students, teachers and parents, Don and Linda raised questions of race, sex and class through workshops, film series and talks. Linda ran a multi-racial girls' video project at the local junior high school where participants were taught hands-on video skills and saw how racism, sexism, and classism affected their daily lives.

In its fifteen years of existence, Basement was supported by the spirit, energy and love of those who believe that change is possible; that visions become realities; that we do and can make a difference in our everyday lives for our communities, our friends, and families, and in our individual journeys through life. Basement's important offshoots have included the New York Chinatown History Project's Library Collection, Asian American Dance Theater, Morita Dance Company, *Bridge*, and the Center for Educational Equity. Much gratitude is owed to the many artists and arts organizations who have participated in Basement's activities over the last fifteen years. When Basement started there was only the beginnings of an Asian American movement and few publicly visible Asian American artists. Now they shine like stars in the universe; we will be surprised by many more.

UP, DOWN, AND BEYOND
THE WEST COAST

ALAN CHONG LAU, SEATTLE (1994)

Outside a crisp rain streaks the window as the smack of tires turning on wet blacktop fills the air. I have scoured my library glancing through improvised bookcases that once held tubers of muddy lotus root and lugs of Orosi peaches to find the oldest Asian American literary volume I possess. Something that would jar memories loose and put faces to names that have faded from memory. It's not *No-No Boy* or *Eat A Bowl of Tea* or even an essay by Sui Sin Far or a poem by Carlos Bulosan. Instead, it's the tattered mimeographed pages found within a faded blue binder labeled "Asian American Studies 117, Spring Semester 1970." This was the first creative writing class I'd ever taken filled with all Asian American students, taught by an Asian American instructor fresh out of graduate school. That teacher was also a fiction writer and his name was Jeffery Paul Chan. I was new to the city having transferred from a strike-torn College of San Mateo only to land at a San Francisco State College hip-deep in student demands for Third World studies.

Staring at my classmates was like placing a mirror in front of my own face. It was a liberating experience for a 19-year-old Chinese American country boy who had grown up in an all-white town. There were others of us from places as far as Hawaii or towns up and down the Sacramento and San Joaquin valleys but by far, most of my classmates came from the Bay Area, where being Asian gave safety in numbers.

It was here I would meet Russell Leong coming to terms with his relationships with family, identity, and sexuality in lyrical haunting poems and essays about the loneliest man in the world, or penning the lyrics to a fortune cookie blues. It was here I would meet an energetic George Leong who would write poems of a real Chinatown I had never lived in. I met Russell Robles, from a large San Francisco Filipino American family, whose older brother Al was a real poet who lived in a temple in Japan studying zen. And it was here I briefly met Sam Tagatac, who was studying filmmaking and writing. More than a writing class, it gave us a chance to talk about our own insecure groping for relationships with family, identity, and a sense of community. Jeff Chan, only ten years older than most of the class, provided an encouraging voice and a sympathetic ear.

I remember sitting over dinner with Jeff and his wife Janet in an apartment somewhere around the Haight sharing a joint as he asked us if we had read Richard Brautigan or met Frank Chin. Chin would prove a pivotal figure for many of us. Brought to San Francisco State by his friend Jeff Chan as a guest lecturer, he would stomp around classes cajoling us to write about ourselves, shouting that there was a distinctive Asian American voice in literature, and that we should express it.

His words were like a brisk slap in the face for many of us and inspired many to begin researching Asian America cultural legacies. During this time, Chin began working on a play entitled "Dear Lo Fan, Honky etc...." He needed a cast and Asian American students on campus were quickly recruited. I think we had a total of three performances before the cast began to fall apart. I remember filmmaker Curtis Choy and I played Chinese gold miners shot to death in the mountains. We had a lot of fun smashing plastic packets of ketchup on our bare chests and screaming "Aiiieeeee!"

During the strike at San Francisco State that threatened to drag on forever, many of the ethnic students began writing poetry and prose expressing their thoughts on the struggle and identity. The San Francisco Poetry Center organized a Third World poetry reading on campus and I think I may have met and read together with the poet Janice Mirikitani at that time. Also the poet Francis Oka who worked at City Lights bookstore began organizing the first Asian American literary magazine entitled *Aion*. I met him on occasion at Asian American student meetings. Kearny Street Workshop formed as a writing collective and rallied around the struggle to save the "I" Hotel in Chinatown not long after. After only taking a couple semesters at San Francisco State, I left for Europe. Ostensibly, the trip was to be best man at my sister's wedding in Copenhagen but I ended up being out of the country for over five years. After a year of traveling and hitchhiking around Europe and across the Middle East to India, I landed in Japan. It was there that I met Japanese poets Yuzuru Katagiri and Yo Nakayama, who had translated many of the Beat poets, such as Ginsburg, Snyder, Rexroth, and later the folkie Bob Dylan. They began having their own readings at local coffeeshops in Kyoto and I would participate. When they helped the poet Kenneth Rexroth settle in Kyoto, they introduced us to each other at Honyarado. I remember the grand poet Rexroth turning to me and saying, "You mean you haven't met Jessica? She's really something else." That was the first time I had heard of San Francisco poet and performer Jessica Hagedorn. It was in Kyoto that I also met the poet Garrett Hongo. He had heard of me from a mutual friend in town and when I was introduced, all he could ask me was "How do you know Frank Chin?" Meeting him for the first time was like being interrogated as he picked my brain about any Asian American writer I ever encountered in the Bay Area. He told me about a fine Japanese American poet in Oregon he had been communicating with and how much he admired his work. It was the first time I had ever heard the name Lawson Inada. It was in Kyoto that I also met the Boston poet Cid Corman, through Garrett. That would introduce me to another side of poetry, as Corman would talk about poets like Creeley, Olson, William Bronk, Basho and René Char with a vigor and depth I had not encountered before.

I returned with my Japanese wife Kazuko to California in 1975, and we settled near Santa Cruz, where both of us ended up returning to school. I went to the first Asian American writer's conference at the Oakland Museum and met dozens of pioneer writers for the first time, including Bill Wu, a science fiction writer from the University of Michigan. I remember meeting Lawson Inada for the first time there. He was a tall man in a tan safari jacket and tie with a Cheshire cat grin that broadened mischievously under a dark moustache as we were introduced. He bellowed to my wife, "Hey. Welcome to my country!" Holding me in a firm handshake he began to chortle, pointing at me with his other hand. "Oh yeah—the monk, the monk. You're the monk I heard about." Something about Lawson's laugh, the way it rumbles from the pit of his stomach and comes out in sunny churning waves of feeling washing over you got me to laughing, too. I must have innocently mentioned in a letter to someone that my father-in-law in Bangkok had taken me along when he visited a friend of his who was a priest at a monastery. In Thailand, it's not uncommon for young boys to spend some time as apprentice monks at Buddhist temples. At any rate, after being out of the country for a few years—Shawn Wong had said that I'd boarded a Greyhound and gone around the world—I guess rumors got started. Other writers at the conference were Hisaye Yamamoto, Janice Mirikitani, Ben Fee, Joaquin Legazpi, Wakako Yamauchi, Sam Tagatac, Oscar Penaranda, Frank Chin, Shawn Wong, Jade Snow Wong, Yoshiko Uchida, Jeanne Wakatsuki Houston, George Leong, Al Robles, Iwao Kawakami, Momoko Iko, Banyani Mariano, Hiroshi Kashiwagi and Emily Cachapero. Also participating in sessions and workshops was poet Doug Yamamoto, who would later help form the Japantown Art and Media workshop (JAM) in San Francisco.

While attending the conference one night I went to a party at Geraldine Kudaka's house. I vaguely remember the sting of marijuana smoke in the air as couples danced to a record of Gil Scott-Heron's "The Bottle." The downstairs neighbors complained about the noise and then the lights went out. As we groped our way down the stairs, we saw Lawson Inada coming up wearing dark sunglasses.

When Japanese poet friend Yuzuru Katagiri came to City Lights to see his old friend Shig Murao I helped him do some book shopping. I piled *No-No Boy* and *Aiiieeeee!* on top of his copy of Bukowski's *Notes of a Dirty Old Man*. Later, our mutual Japanese poet friend Yo Nakayama ended up translating *No-No Boy* into Japanese and it became an underground bestseller praised by the likes of novelist Kenzaburo Oe.

It was while a student at the University of California at Santa Cruz that I met the poet and playwright Lori Higa who was then just graduating, and the novelist Joy Kogawa who was traveling across the country talking to Asian Americans on a Canadian writer's grant. It was there I also met Jaime Jacinto outside a William Everson "Birth of the Poet" class. I was editing an Asian American student magazine started a year earlier by UC Santa Cruz Asian American students entitled "Rising Waters." Jaime looked hip and casually dapper in a gold beret, kerchief tied around his neck, and sporting a backpack . He told me, "Yeah, Brother Antoninus is my main man." I also met a Filipino American couple in my wife's Asian American history class at Cabrillo College, Jeff Tagami and Shirley Ancheta. Both were writing poetry and fiction and studying locally with Kirby Olson, Anita Wilkins, and Joseph Stroud. They would offer to drive us into their hometown of Watsonville after class so we could pick up some fresh tofu at the market. Though they both knew of Carlos Bulosan (a friend of Jeff's mother), they didn't know of many of the more contemporary Asian American writers. I think I loaned them copies of *Aiiieeeee!* and *Yardbird Reader*. They eventually moved to San Francisco and hooked up with Kearny St. Workshop, and later the Filipino American Writers Workshop. At that time Jessica read and almost sang with her group "The Gangster Choir." We would drive up to the Bay Area to see them perform and every time we saw her, there would be a different guitar player. But the music and lyrics would always move us to dance. Evidently, someone at Stanford University knew I was living in California again. On a number of occasions I would be asked to read for Asian American students at their dormitory called "John Okada House." I remember the students being very nice but poor. They never could pay the readers but instead encouraged us to eat as much as we wanted after the reading at the refreshment table. I read with Janice Mirikitani twice and also with Hiroshi Kashiwagi and Jeanne Wakatsuki Houston. I met the Houstons while living in Santa Cruz. I remember one Stanford reading where my mother, father, sister, brother, brother-in-law, and my two nieces came to hear me. They all lived nearby on the peninsula. As I began to read a serious poem about a letter to my father, my whole family began a hopeless struggle to conceal their laughter. Finally my two nieces couldn't hold it any longer and really started laughing. Hearing this, I had to struggle to stop myself from cracking up while reading the serious lines. Later my sister would say, "I couldn't help it Al. I've never heard you sound like that before." My mother couldn't stop saying, "Al, do you know your nostrils enlarge when you read your poems?"

In 1976, Garrett Hongo, Stephen Sumida, and others would put together a Pacific Northwest Asian American writer's conference. It was there I met Northwest poets Jim Mitsui, Laureen Mar, Lonny Kaneko, and Norm Kaneko, as well as visiting writers Milton Murayama, Bienvenido Santos, and N.V.M. Gonzales for the first time. Local poets Al Hikida and Ticang Diangnon were also at the conference.

Shortly after this, Garrett was able to arrange a reading that would put himself, Lawson Inada, and myself in concert with local musicians. The musicians were coordinated by Garrett's younger guitarist brother Eldon and featured sax player Alan Furutani and others. Garrett dubbed our three-poet group, the Buddha Bandits and the concert went pretty well. Afterwards, I discussed with Lawson and Garrett the possibility of doing a book together about our different upbringings along Highway 99. Everyone thought it was a good idea and so on a whim, I submitted a grant proposal to the then newly formed California Arts Commission. Much to our surprise, our proposal received funding. I think one reason we got the grant was because the commission was new and a bureaucracy hadn't had time to set in. It was the bright-eyed optimistic early days of new Governor Jerry Brown's administration. There was also the fact that the commission had members like Ruth Asawa, Gary Snyder, and Peter Coyote who were active artists instead of arts bureaucrats. I would later learn from the radio news that our proposal and that of some Indians' plan to do a rain dance in the Mojave Desert were criticized and deemed frivolous by some members of the capitol legislature.

In 1977, we moved to Seattle and we've been here ever since. While coordinating the International District Street Fair, I met local poets like Sharon Hashimoto, Tina Koyama, Deborah Lee, Kathy Wong, and Bee Bee Tan, most of them referred to me by University of Washington teacher and poet Nelson Bentley. Shawn Wong, who moved to Seattle shortly before I did, introduced me to Shalin Hai-Jew, then a 16-year-old freshperson at UW. I would meet Traise Yamamoto later at a reading introduced to me by Sharon Hashimoto. In 1983, I received an Exchange Artist's Grant from the Japan/US Friendship Commission and the NEA. I was able to spend 9 months in Japan traveling and writing. I later discovered that to my surprise, I was the first Asian American to ever receive this grant though it had been in existence a number of years. Later, dancer Theodora Yoshikami and writers David Mura and Jeanne Wakatsuki Houston would also be recipients. During this time, I was able to go to Hawaii and meet for the first time writers there, such as Wing Tek Lum, Cathy Song, Darrell Lum, Eric Chock, and many others. I've continued to meet writers and poets passing through town to do readings or through correspondence while working on anthologies such as *Turning Shadows Into Light* (with Mayumi Tsutakawa) and the *Contact II* Asian American issue (with Laureen Mar, Winter/Spring 1986). In the early 80's, I also met many Asian Canadian writers, artists and musicians such as Rick Shiomi, Tamio Wakayama, Jim Wong-chu, Mayu Takasaki, Roy Kiyooka, and others, when I read with Lawson Inada. Another time I vaguely remember hearing an Asian American folk group play once at the Ethnic Cultural Center sponsored by Asian American Students. It featured Rick Shiomi on banjo (or was it mandolin?) and as yet relative unknowns David Henry Hwang on violin and Phil Gotanda on guitar and vocals. I remember thinking the violin player seemed to be the best musician amongst them. Mention must be made of Japanese American used bookseller David Ishii. Through the years he has befriended Asian American writers and artists, letting them use his shop for small talk, reading the paper, killing time or fierce debates, and he has always been a loyal supporter and sympathetic listener. He is a friend to all Asian Americans in the arts. Even those who are no longer on speaking terms with each other always talk to David. Through my work at the community newspaper, *International Examiner*, I try to coordinate book review supplements annually that will cover the flood of Asian Pacific American literary titles. Every once in a while, we organize group readings at Elliott Bay Book Co. that involve many of the fine local writers.

• • • • • •

I've been at the computer so long that the morning rain has turned into sunshine. I'm sure I've left a lot out due to my advancing age and rusty memory. Call Jeff Tagami: he can tell you more about Kearny St. Workshop, as can Al Robles and Lou Syquia. Jeff can also fill you in on the Filipino American Writers Workshop. Jessica can tell you about the early multicultural performance scene in San Francisco in the 70s with folks like Ntozake Shange. And Doug Yamamoto can talk about JAM workshop. You should also have someone talk to you about the early *Gidra* days in L.A. Garrett or Lonny Kaneko could fill you in on the early days in the Northwest. Ah, it's endless!

THE BEGINNINGS OF ASIAN AMERICAN POETRY IN HAWAII: A LOCAL VIEWPOINT

ERIC CHOCK, HONOLULU (1994)

Before the 1978 Talk Story conference in Honolulu, while I was helping to organize the *Talk Story Anthology*, I met the poet Wing Tek Lum for the first time over lunch in Chinatown. He called me a "pake," the local term for Chinese in Hawaii. I was confused, wondering if he was somehow using the pejorative sense, meaning that I was cheap, or tight with my money. We didn't even have our food yet, much less the check. And being only half Chinese, I just think of myself as local. But when I told him so, he continued. "You're a pake poet, you wrote 'Manoa Cemetery.'" I had considered the poem about my Chinese grandmother's funeral one of personal mourning and universal themes. He saw ethnicity in the voice of the poem. It was a way of relating I hadn't considered.

In Hawaii, Asian American is a term we learned as adults, not one we grew up with. We used specific ethnic labels—Hawaiian, Japanese, Chinese, Portuguese, Korean, Filipino, et cetera—or "haole," a generic label used for all Caucasians. Or we just thought of ourselves as local people, a mixture of the various groups that grew up here. For me, the term Asian American began to make sense when I became involved with the planning of Talk Story. I was finishing my M.A. in English at the University of Hawaii. All the writers we had studied were white, as were the teachers and almost all the visiting poets. Unlike many universities on the mainland, we had no ethnic literature classes here, unless one means courses in Asian Studies. So we were stunned when almost two hundred

Asian Americans from the mainland attended the Talk Story ethnic writers conference. Talk Story, an academic conference, was attended by hundreds of local people, and (with Maxine Kingston's help) was covered by the press in the context of ongoing ethnic American literary traditions. And given that the majority of our population is Asian/Pacific, I think it is fair to say that it altered the perception and direction of literature in Hawaii. It certainly changed my perspective as a writer.

In all four years of hanging around poetry workshops, it had never been emphasized that an ethnic viewpoint could affect the interpretation of an image in a poem, which was supposedly of the human spirit, whatever one's background. But the one example where a cultural image came into question stood out clearly in my mind. A bearded haole student had written a poem about suddenly seeing a beautiful white crane in a field, in a sort of Americanized version of a Buddhist vision. A local Japanese student, who I found out later was the son of a priest, and who was from a part of the island not far from the rural setting of the poem, was offended that someone would try to pass off a common cattle egret as the white crane of Buddhist literature and art. He couldn't understand why no one cared about the difference, as we muddled over the bird's religious symbolism, and went on.

In hindsight, however, I should say that we were already on our way toward an Asian American literary perspective. We were not so far removed from the mainland as to have been unaware of ethnic movements there. And throughout the 1970's, the Hawaii Literary Arts Council struggled with a rift defined by its Local Writers versus Major Writers reading series: the separate pay scales created the tension, and haole professors versus local writers and students generally defined the two factions. The long-standing "local vs. haole" division in island life carried over into the literary arena. Also, the native Hawaiian movement was already building, noticeably with the occupations on Kaho'olawe in 1976–77. With it came a resurgence of ethnic Hawaiian culture and cultural groups, which many local people supported. But there being no comparable local Asian political issues, there was less need to define any Asian American literary alliances.

During the time of Talk Story, things began to fall into place. I began to understand how Steve Sumida used the same poem that Wing Tek Lum had to place me, and claimed me as being of the same community; and therefore, even though I was a stranger, he could walk up to me on campus and invite me to help with the conference.

I became inspired in my work with the Poets in the Schools program, realizing the importance of providing students with models of poets who had voices sounding like their own, with their various cultural backgrounds being the very guts of their poems, rather than a hindrance to their poetical achievements. I began to see how important it was to provide that sense of multiculturalism so that all writers could feel comfortable in using their most natural voices, instead of trying to conform to some standardized, supposedly absolute ideal.

I began to see how important it was in 1978 for Darrell Lum and myself to start *Bamboo Ridge, The Hawaii Writers' Quarterly*, which has published more contemporary poetry and fiction than any other literary press in Hawaii to date. Perhaps it still survives precisely because it attempts to be representative, embracing the Asian American and the Local, and sustaining its multicultural mission.

It became obvious as I discussed these issues with Sumida, Arnold Hiura, and Marie Hara, of Talk Story Inc., or with Darrell Lum and other Talk Story Anthology staff, that these issues affected many other local writers and educators, and that there was no way we could continue without acknowledging the importance of our ethnic communities in our work. They were not the only influence, but one which could no longer be ignored.

The Talk Story conference discussed traditions of Asian American and local literatures from many different viewpoints. The resonance we felt was unexpected, since most of us had never been taught that we would be able to see ourselves so completely in the characters and voices and images of literature. We saw that the local point of view which we were writing from was still developing, but—using our cultural backgrounds—it was as legitimate and important as any other. And it was wonderful to feel someone appreciate the cultural aspects for what they really were. For someone trained on white mainstream culture, it was a kind of literary reassurance laying the groundwork for us as writers to explore and use local topics in our work to an extent which, especially in poetry, had not been done before. With Talk Story, we created a new vision of ourselves. It was then up to us to fulfill it.

The lessons of Talk Story were reinforced the following year when we got Frank Chin to be a visiting writer. He stayed for a month at the home of Wing Tek Lum, and gave various talks, workshops, interviews, readings, and classes. He met informally with a small group of interested local Asian writers every night talking literature and culture. Everything was interpreted culturally: food, dress, music, movies, slang, dating, drinking, everything. He was adamant that culture and cultural values are conveyed in our language and literature, and he insisted that, in contrast to the negative or limited stereotypes in the American mass media, we should be able to draw upon and continue the Asian and Asian American heroic traditions that engender pride in one's ethnic background, instead of perpetuating the message that we are in many ways inferior to white American culture. His message was that much of American literature and the way it is taught is historically prejudiced against ethnic minorities, and that we should be willing to fight to uphold our ethnic pride.

The month after he left, when the Hawaii Literary Arts Council held its annual elections, there was a so-called "coup." A group of local (Asian and haole) writers petitioned and campaigned against a slate of nominees that basically represented the mainland-born, University of Hawaii academic faction that had dominated the council. I was president, Muffy Webb, a local haole, vice-president, and Wing Tek Lum, treasurer. We—and this includes members of Talk Story, the Bamboo Ridge study group, and others—began to change the direction of the literary activities in the state, the Council being the only state-wide funding organization for literary activities.

We began to have a new position of leverage with the State Foundation of Culture and the Arts as well. We began sponsoring a more multi-ethnic list of visiting writers. Talk Story and Bamboo Ridge began to get state funding for projects. During the next year after Talk Story, Stephen Sumida and Arnold Hiura researched the first ethnic bibliography in Hawaii, *Asian American Literature of Hawaii*. The ideas of multicultural literature broached at Talk Story, and reinforced by Frank Chin's visit, began to trickle into the University of Hawaii English department through the inclusion of some local writers in class syllabi. The *Talk Story Anthology* itself appeared on several UH reading lists. The English Department briefly offered an Asian American literature course (but now has none). Even certain members of the state Department of Education began to look at local literature for possible inclusion in class curricula. The UH English department honored Maxine Hong Kingston, Lawson Inada, Bienvenido Santos, and, later, Cathy Song as visiting writers for one semester stints, but as yet there are no local or Asian American writers on the permanent faculty. There were follow-up conferences including two more by Talk Story Inc., and the Writers of Hawaii conference, among others. In many ways, it can be said that a gradual, steady blooming of local literature has continued since Talk Story, as Hawaii has become more accepting of its own writers, and non-canonical or ethnic writing in general.

In the years since Talk Story, there have been many Asian American poets in Hawaii, but as an editor here all those years it is interesting to me that those few who have gone on to publish books are all now associated with the Bamboo Ridge study group: Wing Tek Lum, Cathy Song, Juliet Kono, Lois-Ann Yamanaka, and myself. Song, the only one to publish successfully with an established mainland poetry press, has her third book due in 1994. Wing Tek Lum continues his development of historical Asian

American themes, writing poems on the early Chinese in Hawaii. Kono has expanded her Hilo plantation subject matter, both in short stories and in a manuscript of poems about the tsunami which devastated the Big Island in her childhood. She also has a sonnet sequence based on living with a relative with Alzheimer's Disease. Yamanaka, whose first book, *Saturday Night at the Pahala Theater*, was released in 1993, deals with topics of sexuality and abuse in a strong pidgin voice unlike any other heard before.

Although our literary network in Hawaii is not large, it is healthy. It has helped our cause that Cathy Song won the Yale Series of Younger Poets prize, and that Wing Tek Lum, Garrett Hongo, and Fred Baysa have won the Nation's Discovery Award. Perhaps it helps that some local news writers were actually at the Talk Story conference, or read the *Talk Story Anthology* and *Bamboo Ridge* while studying at the UH. It has helped our cause that the national Association for Asian American Studies has given Book of the Year Awards to four Bamboo Ridge Press publications: *Expounding the Doubtful Points* by Wing Tek Lum; *Pass On, No Pass Back* by Darrell Lum; *The Watcher of Waipuna* by Gary Pak; and *Saturday Night at the Pahala Theater* by Lois-Ann Yamanaka. We have been able to accomplish that feat, in part, because after Frank Chin left we began a writers' study group which has met monthly since 1980 to study our Asian American literary roots and fellow writers, as well as to workshop our own new work. It helps our cause that Bamboo Ridge Press— working from connections established through Talk Story and the Poets in the Schools program—has a local literature workshop series for teachers of the state, which provides them an opportunity to discover poems and stories which their students may find more relevant. It has helped our cause in the fifteen years since Talk Story that we have continued to sponsor visits by leading Asian American writers from the mainland each year. We have been doing our homework and keeping track of all our literary roots in America, and we hope that those on the mainland will keep us in mind as they do the same.

WORD

KIMIKO HAHN, NEW YORK (1994)

The first reading I ever gave was at Basement Workshop, then several flights above Catherine Street. This was 1982. Jessica Hagedorn lined me up with a poet I'd never met and who has become over the years an important and trusted friend, Sekou Sundiata. That was Basement: performances, connections, waves of dissonance. And always "multicultural," not for the fund, but for the fun: political and aesthetic.

Sekou's voice was so steady it rocked my heart. His politics so quietly clear, my head fused. From confusion, fusion.

When Fay Chiang dropped the reins, and Teddy Yoshikami and Jessica moved on, the filmmakers Chris Choy and Renee Tajima asked if I'd continue Basement Workshop's reading series. The first one I put together, at Cobi's on Lafayette Street, coyly presented Jessica's fiction (she was still best known for her poetry then) and Diana Chang's poetry in between an Asian American jazz spot and fashion show. Of course it was hot.

That moment in Manhattan was post-American Writer's Congress (2500 writers at a historic meeting in October, 1981) and pre-Artists Call (unprecedented rallying of artists against U.S. intervention in Central America); *Bridge: Asian American Perspectives* had been revived with a new focus thanks to the collective effort of, among others, Renee, Walter, David Low, Marsha Tajima, and myself. A couple of important organizations were hanging in (such as the Chinatown History Project and Asian American Arts Centre), although none sponsored readings. Word events ebbed. I was in between marriages, circulating the manuscript of my first full collection of poetry, and trying to cut loose all academic ties. To climb out of the dictionary:

4309   GEN, GON word
F1726

4313   KO get confused
F1729

To translate radical (the root part of a Chinese character) to radical, as in subversion. Public servants were just beginning to cut back the arts, an economic slash we would soon experience politically in the Reagan-Bush homophobic, anti-woman, anti-civil rights, give-back, union-busting, philistinian era. The beginning of the real estate boom, the beginning of homelessness as we live with it today. Funding for Asian American arts was cut back especially since there was no major institutional support; at the same time, Asian American artists were wooed by institutions savvy enough to hear "multicultural" as the coming buzz word. Basement knew the numbers. Any "minority" organization knew it.

The second year, as Word of Mouth, Quynh Thai of Film News Now Foundation (the parent organization) further professionalized the reading series. The Chatham Square Public Library in Chinatown continued co-sponsorship by hosting the programs in their third-floor loft, upgraded the sound system and (after Manuel Ramos Otero boomed, "do it the way I tell you to or don't do it at all.") soundproofed the room. Magnificent Manhattan space. Free. Just walk in.

Favorite readings? Shawn Wong, Thought Music, Quincey Troupe, Diana Davenport, Ai, Jack Hirschman, Li-Young Lee, Patricia Jones—and the most Inspiring and Important, Hisaye Yamamoto who traveled by train from Los Angeles and finally met Yuri and Bill Kochiyama. The two women had heard of each other but never met back in the internment camps. We got money to bring folks in and we did.

I did Word for about three years. Trinh Minh-ha, in one of my last seasons, to a standing-room-only crowd, read from her *Woman Native Other*, a classic before it hit the bookstores, libraries and classrooms. Did she read this portion: "Power, as unveiled by numerous contemporary writings, has always inscribed itself in language. Speaking, writing and discoursing are not mere acts of communication; they are above all acts of compulsion. Please follow me."?

Across the street at Asian CineVision, Jessica and Darryl Chin ran a series called "Talk'n'Cheap" where writers led discussions—David Henry Hwang read from M. Butterfly before it opened on Broadway. The Asian American Studies Association held its annual conference in New York in 1989 and the Asian American Arts Alliance was born. All this despite continued cutbacks.

With a second baby on the way, I left the project to poet Indran Amirthanayagam. At that point, the projects had to be scaled back, no surprise, due to "freezes and cuts." For several of the last programs he was able to hook up with the Academy of American Poets Asian American tours. Economic constraints dictated the content of culture, business as usual.

Nowadays, new organization, the Asian American Writers' workshop has thrust a group of young writers into leadership positions. Their program offers peer workshops, a "moveable" reading series, fellowships, a journal, and contests. And the Asian American Arts Alliance held a national conference in New York.

A new skin. Of course.

HERE, NOT THERE

GERRY SHIKATANI, MONTRÉAL (1994)

Just the thought of speaking about, of shaping my own words around, this sense of a poetry come from Canadians of Asian ancestry, is so foreign to the way poetry has existed up to now in Canada. Not that I don't stumble about in such a sense, of gathering, collecting, in my experience as a poet, this process (face to face of it all, brother and sister slant-eye eh, the faces and names one recognizes—Orientals, we, the other side of the Pacific). But the naming, describing/ascribing (the critical writing ergo canonization) of 'Asian-Canadian literature' which can proffer that sense of a fixed concept, of a valid telling of the Canadian vision does not exist, is silent. In a sense, as collective, we exist in zero, dependent on the Canadian canon.

(Back in 1981, when David Aylward and I edited *Paper Doors: An Anthology of Japanese-Canadian Poetry*, which included poems in English and Japanese, we had been supported by Coach House Press editor bpNichol and received wonderful, generous backcover blurbs and support from Robert Weaver and Eli Mandel, two major senior figures in the Canadian literary establishment. Only one major newspaper and no national popular magazine reviewed the book.)

Poem-making is a marginalized activity (and I emphasize this passive), and oh how it's easy once one chooses this way, to yield to the larger community, to play a part in the country's literary culture. It seems at least acceptable to many of us, if not achievement, a privileged class. Membership, ah membership &, we are convinced.

But to speak of Asian-Canadian etc.!? How unusual ne!? One simply, one simply doesn't hear such pronouncements from those authorities who define Canadian poetry through the vehicles of criticism, theory, and other scholarship.

And I think that here, reviewers, critics—in the news, journals—are noticeably silent about a poetry of Canadians of our rice and soya sauce selves. But from where I sit, I see this language as peculiarly our own and its strength is to hold to its own inherent validity not as some addendum or marginal trunkline of "Canadian Poetry."

Oh, we haven't been abundant, those who have been writing and publishing poetry for some time. There are some of South Asian descent, few of Chinese (the best known, Fred Wah whose father's father came from Canton), some of Japanese—and only two or three rarely published poets who are from Korean or Southeast Asian Canadian worlds. The late Roy Kiyooka, Fred Wah and Joy Kogawa (now more reknowned as a novelist) have been the most recognized and published. When I began this rigour, they'd been attending to it already for some time. Where I could hinge.

And what strikes me as quite amazing is that for such a small group of writers, the writing from those like Roy, Fred, and Joy has a disproportionately large significance in the literature made in Canada. And amazing too, how so much of the writing by Roy, Fred, then myself, and now Roy Miki, and now some emerging poets has been engaged in a specific kind of language process and view: less linear anecdotal, and distinct from the centrifugal pump of convention. So much of the poetry has not been narratives "about" the Asian Canadian experience per se, though they circulate through and within it.

> "got" his eyes, sister
> after the brothers
> genetic it, you
> left
> with your own fatherness
> > (from "Breathin' My Name
> > With A Sigh." Fred Wah)

The poetry I'm talking about is one which has been true to its sense of experience of language as breath, tongue, as we are the body of the perceived "other," and hasn't accepted the writing forms and conduit systems of mainstream culture to simply tell the desired story of "minority experience," as snapshot. There's a real attention to the concrete details of living to create a certain place of language, of notation where there is the possibility of writing what is not, rather than fulfilling the formulae which repeat in anthology after anthology of Canadian poetry.

Look at poem-making in the hands of people like Roy Kiyooka and Fred: there's a scrupulous attention to the shape of language and music from the heart, which a few other experimenting Canadian poets, such as Phyllis Webb, Steven Smith, Michael Ondaatje, Maxine Gold, and Daphne Marlatt, have also held in high esteem, and to whom we have been likened.

I first came upon Fred and Roy's work through books published by Talon in Vancouver and Coach House Press in Toronto, which back in the 60's and 70's was publishing the most interesting and innovative poetry. A lot of the activity expressed an East-West, Toronto-Vancouver connection, which had a lot to do with poets in touch with, among other things, Beat and Black Mountain poets and that whole attention to breath, proprioception, kinetics and the particulars of local place. And there was Wah, a founder of the *Tish* journal group of poets in Vancouver. There was also the presence of folks like teacher/critic Warren Tallman, and visits by Robert Creeley and Robert Duncan. I remember Ginsberg publishing at Coach House as well.

Eventually, Wah would go study with Creeley, and then Charles Olson, but that's a general picture of Kiyooka and Wah at the time, where they found a place to write, read, and publish. Roy and especially Fred are now highly esteemed (more often by other poets than the editor/scholars, and clearly more in Western Canada), but they are generally regarded in terms of Anglo-centred orbits, not as extraordinary poets who have come out of an Asian physicality and breath. (The very fine critical work on Wah by Pamela Banting is one exception I am aware of; see "The Undersigned:

Ethnicity and Signature—Effects in Fred Wah's Poetry," *West Coast Line*, #2, Fall, 1990). Nevertheless, this relationship to alternative writing has continued. It's in the place of post-modern aesthetics through to language-centred work that the lines of relationship have continued, whether by the intentions of the poets or not. Poets such as the late bpNichol, who never conceded to "Canadian poetry" as a fixed centre of power, but engaged in process, the actualization of the many, have been the consistent readers of our work. It's where this writing has found home and listener in Canada, and brought recognition to Wah and Kiyooka.

It is true, Wah's volume of poetry *Waiting For Saskatchewan* was awarded the Governor-General's Award for 1985 (Canada's top annually awarded literary prizes) and Roy Kiyooka was short-listed for his *Pear Tree Pomes* in 1987. Still, Fred is found in too few anthologies, Roy almost never. Too many Canadian poets have barely read him. Joy Kogawa's poems have not been seen as part of this kind of writing, but are, in my hearing, distinct and of the Nisei—poems rich with small ephemera and an understated sometimes discontinuous voice:

> and there the camera and—
> Click, the latch. Click
> the tiny language of
> terror. Don't
> go please, he
> says, without at least
> breakfast.
>
> (from "Parting Shots")

Her novel *Obasan* has brought her acclaim, but her poetry has been bypassed. So here, in Kiyooka and Wah, and to a lesser extent Joy, I'm speaking about major poets who have given real shape to the language of the geography they stand in, but have not been given the same unequivocal attention as Caucasian writers of their achievement.

All of this art seems to me about a meticulous attention to, and wanting fidelity to our breaths, our "yellow" bodies, our gestural paths. We write to activate language as we hear it. This isn't ordinary stuff and I wonder why this first generation of Canook writers we are don't seem to get the words out in a straight way—why those main tracks just don't feel right—and so we move with our own planes and shifts.

And as I'm writing this now, there is more happening on many fronts. A new generation of writers across the country, especially in Vancouver where I've been amazed by the sheer positive exuberance of Chinese Canadian writers. Roy Miki is leading the emergence of criticism, theory, and scholarship around Asian Canadians writing from within the community—a group of Japanese Canadians are among his students at Simon Fraser University in Vancouver. He is also an editor for the journal *West Coast Line*, teaming up with Fred Wah, who's at the University of Calgary influencing a new important generation of writers/editors, such as Ashok Mathur.

So the sensibility continues its swim outside the suck of the tidal current, asserts itself at the marginal lines. But in standing here and now, the strength of it is where the breath is rooted, here and not there, in a space of wanting, claiming this water as the centre of language and the making of poems.

ASIAN AMERICAN POETRY: A BIBLIOGRAPHY

SINGLE AUTHOR VOLUMES

Abe, Ryan. *Golden Sunrises-A Narrative Haiku*. San Mateo, CA.: Farris Press, 1973.

Ai. *Cruelty*. Boston: Houghton Mifflin, 1973.

Ai. *Fate*. Boston: Houghton Mifflin, 1991.

Ai. *Greed*. New York: W.W. Norton and Co., 1995.

Ai. *Killing Floor*. Boston: Houghton Mifflin, 1979.

Ai. *Sin*. New York: Houghton Mifflin Company, 1986.

Akiyoshi, Dennis. *Poetry*. Los Angeles: International Publication, 1984.

Alexander, Meena. *The Bird's Bright Ring*. Calcutta Writers Workshop, 1976.

Alexander, Meena. *House of a Thousand Doors*. Washington: Three Continents Press, 1987.

Alexander, Meena. *I Root My Name*. Calcutta: United Writers, 1977.

Alexander, Meena. *Stone Roots*. New Dehli: Arnold-Heinemann, 1980.

Alexander, Meena. *The Storm*. New York: Red Dust, 1989.

Alexander, Meena. *Without Place*. Calcutta: Writers Workshop, 1977.

Ali, Agha Shahid. *A Nostalgist's Map of America*. New York: W.W. Norton, 1991.

Ali, Agha Shahid. *A Walk Through the Yellow Pages*. Tucson, Arizona: SUN/gemini Press, Inc., 1987.

Amirthanayagam, Indran. *The Elephants of Reckoning*. Brooklyn: Hanging Loose Press, 1993.

Angeles, Carlos A. *A Stun of Jewels*. Manila: Alberto S. Florentino, 1963.

Bannerji, Himani. *A Separate Sky*. Toronto: Domestic Bliss Press, 1982.

Bergonio, Gemma. *Mirror at Dawn*. City of Industry, CA: Ted A Villagonas, L.A.C. Publishing, 1985.

Berssenbrugge, Mei-mei. *Empathy*. Barrytown, NY: Station Hill Press, 1989.

Berssenbrugge, Mei-mei. *Fish Souls*. New York: Greenwood, 1971.

Berssenbrugge, Mei-mei. *The Heat Bird*. Providence: Burning Deck Press, 1983.

Berssenbrugge, Mei-mei. *Packrat Sieve*. Bowling Green, New York: Contact II, 1983.

Berssenbrugge, Mei-mei. *Random Possession*. New York: I. Reed Books, 1979.

Berssenbrugge, Mei-mei. *Sphericity*. Berkeley: Kelsey St. Press, 1993.

Berssenbrugge, Mei-mei. *Summits Move with the Tide*. Greenfield, New York: Greenfield Review Press, 1974.

Bhaggiyadatta, Krisantha Sri. *Domestic Bliss*. Toronto: Domestic Bliss Press, 1982.

Bhatt, Sujata. *Brunizem*. London: Carcanet Press, 1988.

Bui-Tien-Kohoi [Huy-Luc]. *America, My First Feelings: Poems*. Houston: privately printed, 1981.

Bulosan, Carlos. *Dark People*. Los Angeles, CA.: Wagon Star, 1944.

Bulosan, Carlos. *If You Want to Know What We Are: A Carlos Bulosan Reader*. Minneapolis: West End Press, 1983.

Bulosan, Carlos. *Letters From America*. Prairie City, IL.: J.A. Decker, 1942.

Bulosan, Carlos. *The Voice of Bataan*. New York: Coward-McCann, Inc., 1943.

Caigoy, Faustino. *Bitter Sweet Chocolate Meat*. Los Angeles: Inner City Cultural Center, 1974.

Carbo, Nick. *El Grupo McDonald's*. Chicago: Tia Chucha Press, 1995.

Cerenio, Virginia. *Trespassing Innocence*. San Francisco: Kearny Street Workshop Press.

Chandra, G.S. Sharat. *Aliens*. Safford, AZ: Scattershot Press, 1986.

Chandra, G.S. Sharat. *April in Nanjangud*. London: London Magazine, 1971.

Chandra, G.S. Sharat. *Bharat Natyam Dancer*. Calcutta: Writers Workshop, 1968.

Chandra, G.S. Sharat. *The Ghost of Meaning*. Lewiston, ID: Confluence Press, 1983.

Chandra, G.S. Sharat. *Heirloom*. Delhi: Oxford UP, 1982.

Chandra, G.S. Sharat. *Offsprings of Servagna*. Calcutta: Writers Workshop, 1975.

Chandra, G.S. Sharat. *Once or Twice*. Sutton, Surrey: Hippopotamus Press, 1975.

Chandra, G.S. Sharat. *Will This Forest*. Milwaukee, WI: Morgan Press, 1969.

Chang, Diana. *The Horizon is Definitely Speaking*. New York: Backstreet Editions, 1982.

Chang, Diana. *What Matisse is After*. New York: Contact II, 1984.

Cha, Theresa Hak Kyung. *Dictee*. New York: Tanam Press, 1982.

Cheng, Sait Chia. *Turned Clay*. Fredericton, NB: Fiddlehead Poetry Books, 1981.

Chiang, Fay. *In the City of Contradictions*. New York: Sunbury Press, 1979.

Chiang, Fay. *Miwa's Song*. New York: Sunbury Press, 1983.

Chin, Marilyn. *Dwarf Bamboo*. New York: The Greenfield Review Press, 1987.

Chin, Marilyn. *The Phoenix Gone, The Terrace Empty*. Minneapolis: Milkweed Editions, 1994.

Chinn, Daryl Ngee. *Soft Parts of the Back*. Florida: University of Central Florida Press, 1989.

Chock, Eric. *Last Days Here*. Honolulu: Bamboo Ridge Press, 1990.

Chock, Eric. *Ten Thousand Wishes*. Honolulu: Bamboo Ridge Press, 1978.

Concepcion, Marcelo de Gracia. *Azucena*. New York: Putnam's, 1925.

Concepcion, Marcelo de Gracia. *Bamboo Flute*. Manila: Community Book, 1932.

Crusz, Rienzi. *Elephant and Ice*. Erin, ON: Porcupine's Quill, 1985.

Crusz, Rienzi. *Flesh and Thorn*. Stratford, ON: Pasdeloup Press, 1974.

Crusz, Rienzi. *Singing Against the Wind*. Erin, ON: Porcupine's Quill, 1985.

Crusz, Rienzi. *A Time for Loving*. Toronto: TSAR, 1986.

Dabydeen, Cyril. *Coastland: New and Selected Poems* (1973-1989). Oakville: Mosaic Press, 1989.

Dabydeen, Cyril. *Distances*. Fredericton, N.B: Fiddlehead Poetry Books, 1977.

Dabydeen, Cyril. *Elephants Make Good Stepladders*. London, ON: Third Eye, 1982.

Dabydeen, Cyril. *Goatsong*. Oaksville, ON: Mosaic Press/Valley Editions, 1977.

Dabydeen, Cyril. *Heart's Frame*. Cornwall, ON: Vesta, 1979.

Dabydeen, Cyril. *Islands Lovelier than a Vision*. Yorkshire, Eng.: Peepal Tree Press, 1986.

Dabydeen, Cyril. *Poems in Recession*. Georgetown, Guyana: Sadeek Press, 1972.

Dabydeen, Cyril. *They Call This Planet Earth*. Ottawa: Borealis Press, 1979.

Da Silva, Marion. *Faces Of Life*. Toronto: Mission Press, 1982.

Day, Stacey B. *Poems and Etudes*. Montreal: Cultural and Educational Productions, 1968.

Day, Stacey B. *Ten Poems and a Letter from America for Mr.Sinha*. Montreal: Cultural and Educational Productions, 1971.

Divakaruni, Chitra. *Dark Like the River*. Calcutta: Writers Workshop Press, 1987.

Divakaruni, Chitra. *The Reason for Nasturtiums*. Berkeley: Berkeley Workshop Press, 1990.

Divakaruni, Chitra. *Black Candle*. Corvallis, OR: Calyx Books, 1991.

Du Tu Le. *Tho' Tinh (Love Poem)*. Orange County, CA: Tu sach van hoc Nhan chung Hoa Ky, 1984.

Foo, Josephine. *Endou*. Providence, RI: Los Roads Press, 1995.

Foster, Sesshu. *Angry Days*. Los Angeles: West End Press, 1987.

Fujita, Jun. *Tanka: Poems in Exile*. Chicago: Covic Co., 1923.

Fukaya, Michiyo Cornwell. *Lesbian Lyrics*. New York: Self-published c/o A.L.O.E.C., 1981.

Furuta, Soichi. *To Breathe*. Westbury, NY: Edition Heliodor, 1980.

Francia, Luis. *The Arctic Archipelago*. Manila: Office of Research and Publications of Manila University, 1991.

Francia, Luis. *Her Beauty Likes Me Well*. New York: Petrarch, 1979.

Furtado, R[aul] de L. *The Oleanders*. Calcutta: Writers Workshop, 1968.

Ghose, Zulfikar. *Jets from Orange*. London: Macmillan, 1967.

Ghose, Zulfikar. *The Loss of India*. London: Routledge, 1964.

Ghose, Zulfikar. *A Memory of Asia: New and Selected Poems*. Austin, TX: Curbstone Publishing, 1984.

Ghose, Zulfikar. *The Violent West*. London: Macmillan, 1972.

Gill, Darshan. *Man and the Mirror*. Surrey, BC: Indo-Canadian Publishers, 1976.

Gill, Lakshmi. *During Rain, I Plant Chrysanthemums*. Toronto: Ryerson Press, 1972.

Gill, Lakshmi. *First Clearing*. Manila: Estaniel Press, 1972.

Gill, Lakshmi. *Mind Walls*. Fredericton, NB: Fiddlehead Poetry Books, 1970.

Gill, Lakshmi. *Novena to St. Jude Thaddeus*. Fredericton, NB: Fiddlehead Poetry Books, 1979.

Gill, Stephen M. *Moans and Waves*. Cornwall, ON: Vesta, 1982.

Gill, Stephen M. Reflections: *A Collection of Poems*. Cornwall, ON: Rytes, 1972.

Gill, Stephen M. *Reflections and Wounds*. Cornwall, ON: Vesta, 1978.

Gill, Stephen M. *Wounds: A Collection of Poems*. Cornwall, ON: Vesta, 1974.

Gool, Resahrd. *"In Medusa's Eye" and Other Poems*. Charlottetown, PE: Square Deal Publications, 1972.

Gotera, Vince. *Dragonfly*. San Antonio: Pecan Grove Press, 1994.

Hagedorn, Jessica. "The Death of Anna May Wong." In

Four Young Women: Poems, Ed. Kenneth Peyroth. New York: McGraw, 1973.

Hagedorn, Jessica. *Dangerous Music*. San Francisco: Momo's Press, 1975.

Hagedorn, Jessica. *Danger and Beauty*. New York: Penguin Books, 1993.

Hagedorn, Jessica. *Pet Food and Tropical Apparitions*. San Francisco: Momo's Press, 1981.

Hahn, Kimiko. *Air Pocket*. Brooklyn, NY: Hanging Loose Press, 1989.

Hahn, Kimiko. *Earshot*. Brooklyn, NY: Hanging Loose Press, 1992.

Hahn, Kimiko. *The Unbearable Heart*. New York: Kaya Production, 1995.

Handa, Masao. *I Am A Firefly and Other Poems*. Self-published, 1928.

Hardev. *Doodles and Scribbles*. London, ON: Shabd Publications, 1978.

Hartman, Yuki. *Hot Footsteps*. New York: Telephone Books, 1976.

Hartman, Yuki. *A One of Me*. Genesis, NY: Grasp Press, 1970.

Hartman, Yuki. *Ping*. New York: Kulchur Foundation, 1984.

Hartman, Yuki. *Red Rice: Poems*. Putnam Valley, NY: Swollen Magpie, 1980.

Hartmann, [Carl] Sadakichi. *"Drifting Flowers of the Sea" and Other Poems to Elizabeth Blanche Walsh*. N.p.:n.p., 1904 [Manifold copy.]

Hartmann, [Carl] Sadakichi. *Japanese Rhythms, Tanka, Haik{ai} and Other Forms Translated, Adapted or Imitated by Sadakichi Hartmann.....* N.p.:n.p., 1926.

Hartmann, [Carl] Sadakichi. *My Rubaiyat*. St. Louis: Mangan Printing, 1913. New York: G. Bruno, 1916.

Hartmann, [Carl] Sadakichi. *Naked Ghosts: Four Poems*. South Pasadena, CA: Fantasia, 1925.

Hartmann, [Carl] Sadakichi. *Tanka and Haiku: 14 Japanese*

Rhythms. New York: G. Bruno, 1915.

Hongo, Garrett, et. al. *The Buddha Bandits Down Highway 99*. Mountain View, Cali.: Buddhahead Press, 1978.

Hongo, Garrett. *Yellow Light*. Middletown, Conn.: Wesleyan University Press, 1982.

Hongo, Garrett. *The River of Heaven*. New York: Knopf, 1988.

Honma, Dean. *Night Dive*. Honolulu: Petronium Press, 1985.

Hsia, Wei-Lin. *The Poetry of English and Chinese*. New York: Vantage, 1978.

Ikeda, Patricia. *House of Wood, House of Salt*. Cleveland: Cleveland State University Poetry Center, 1978.

Imura, Ernest Sakayuki. *Sunrise-Sunset*. New York: Vantage, 1976.

Inada, Lawson. *Before the War: Poems as they Happened*. New York: William Morrow and Co., 1971.

Inada, Lawson. *Legends from Camp*. Minneapolis: Coffee House Press, 1992.

Itani, Frances. *No Other Lodgings*. Fredericton, N.B.: Fiddlehead Press, 1978.

Itwaru, Arnold. *Shattered Songs: A Journey from Somewhere to Somewhere*. Toronto: Aya Press, 1982.

Kagawa, Bunichi. *Hidden Flame*. Stanford: Half Moon Press, 1930.

Kageyama, Yuri. *Peeling*. Berkeley, CA: I. Reed Books, 1988.

Kakugawa, Frances. *Sand Grains*. San Antonio: Naylor, 1970.

Kakugawa. Frances. *Golden Spike*. San Antonio: Naylor, 1976.

Kakugawa, Frances. *Path of Butterflies*. San Antonio: Naylor, 1976.

Kakugawa, Frances. *Winter Ginger Blossom*. San Antonio: Naylor, 1971.

Kalsey, Surjeet. *Speaking to the Winds*. London, ON: Third Eye Publications, 1982. Translation.

Kaneko, Lonny. *Coming Home from Camp*. Waldron Island,

WA.: Brooding Heron Press, 1986.

Kanno, Takeshi. *Creation-Dawn*. Fruitvale, CA: The Hights/Self-published, 1913.

Kawakami, Iwao. *The Parents and Other Poems*. San Francisco: Nichibei Times, 1947.

Kim, Allison. *Mirror, Mirror*. Santa Cruz, CA.: Dancing Bird Press, 1986

Kim, Chungmi. *Chungmi*. Anaheim: Korean Pioneer Press, 1982.

Kim, Myung Mi. *Under Flag*. Berkeley: Kelsey St. Press, 1991.

Kim, Willyce. *Under a Rolling Sky*. n.p.: Maude Gonne Press, 1976.

Kim, Willyce. *Eating Artichokes*. Oakland, CA.: The Women's Press Collective, 1972.

Kiyooka, Roy. *Transcanada Letter*. Vancouver, B.C.: Talon Press, 1975.

Kiyooka, Roy. *The Fountainebleu Dream Machine*. Toronto: Coach House, 1967.

Kiyooka, Roy. *Kyoto Airs*. Vancouver: Talonbooks, 1975.

Kiyooka, Roy. *Stoned Gloves*. Toronto: Coach House, 1971.

Kiyooka, Roy. *Wheels*. Toronto: Coach House, 1982.

Ko, Sung-Won. *With Birds of Paradise*. Los Angeles: Azalea Press, 1984.

Ko, Sung-Won. *The Turn of Zero*. New York: Cross-Cultural Communications, 1974.

Kogawa, Joy. *A Choice of Dreams*. Toronto: McClelland & Stewart, 1974.

Kogawa, Joy. *Jerricho Road*. Toronto: McClelland & Stewart, 1977.

Kogawa, Joy. *The Splintered Moon*. NB, Canada: Fiddlehead, 1969.

Kogawa, Joy. *Woman in the Woods*. Ontario, Canada: Mosaic Press, 1985.

Kono, Juliet S. *Hilo Rains*. Honolulu: Bamboo Ridge Press, 1988.

Kono, Juliet S. *Tsunami Years*. Honolulu: Bamboo Ridge Press, 1995.

Kudaka, Geraldine. *Numerous Avalanches at the Point of Intersection*. New York: Greenfield Press, 1979.

Kuo, Alexander. *Changing the River*. Berkeley: Reed & Cannon, 1986.

Kuo, Alexander. *New Letters from Hiroshima*. New York: Greenfield Review Press, 1974.

Kuo, Alexander. *The Window Tree*. Peterborough, NH.: Windy Row Press, 1971.

Kwan, Moon. *A Chinese Mirror*. Los Angeles: Phoenix Press, 1932.

Lai, Him Mark, et. al., ed. *Island*. San Francisco: Hoc Doi, 1980.

Langworthy, Christian Nguyen. *The Geography of War*. Oklahoma City: Cooper House Publishing Inc., 1995.

Larsen, Wendy Wilder, and Tran Thi Nga. *Shallow Graves: Two Women and Vietnam*. New York: Random, 1986.

Lau, Alan Chong. *Songs for Jadina*. New York: Greenfield Review Press, 1980.

Lau, Carolyn. *Wode Shuofa (My Way of Speaking)*. Santa Fe: Tooth of Time, 1988.

Lau, Evelyn. *In the House of Slaves*. Toronto: Coach House Press, 1994.

Lau, Evelyn. *Oedipal Dreams*. Victoria: Beach Holme, 1992.

Lau, Evelyn. *You Are Not Who You Claim*. Victoria: Press Porcepic, 1992.

Lee, Li-Young. *Rose*. Brockport, NY: BOA Editions, 1986.

Lee, Li-Young. *The City in Which I Love You*. Brockport, NY: BOA Editions, 1990.

Lee, Mary. *The Guest of Tyn-y-Coed Cae: Poems and Drawings*. Santa Monica, CA: Hightree Books, 1973.

Lee, Mary. *Hand in Hand*. Illus. author. New York: Crown, 1971.

Lee, Mary. *Tender Bough*. New York: Crown, 1969.

Lee, Mary Wong. *Through My Windows*. Stockton,CA.:

Roxene Lee Publishing, 1970.

Lee, Mary Wong. *Through My Windows, Book II*. Stockton, CA.: Mills Press, 1980.

Lem, Carol. *Don't Ask Why*. Los Angeles: Peddler Press, 1982.

Lem, Carol. *Grassroots*. Los Angeles: Peddler Press, 1975.

Leong, George. *A Lone Bamboo Doesn't Come From Jackson Street*. San Francisco: Isthmus Press, 1977.

Leong, Russell. *In the Country of Dreams and Dust*. Albuquerque: West End Press, 1993.

Lim, Genny. *Winter Place*. San Francisco: Kearny Street Workshop Press.

Lim, Shirley. *Crossing the Peninsula*. Kuala Lumpur: Heinemann, 1980.

Lim, Shirley. *No Man's Grove*. Singapore: National Univ. of Singapore English Dept. Press, 1985.

Lim, Shirley Geok-lin. Modern Secrets. London: Dangaroo Press, 1989.

Lim-Wilson, Fatima. Crossing the Snow Bridge. Columbus: Ohio State University Press, 1995.

Ling, Amy. *Chinamerican Reflections: A Chapbook of Poems and Paintings*. Lewiston, ME: Great Raven Press, 1984.

Liu, Stephen. *Dream Journeys to China*. Beijing: New World Press, 1982.

Liu, Timothy. *Burnt Offerings*. Port Townsend, Washington: Copper Canyone Press, 1995.

Liu, Timothy. *Vox Angelica*. Cambridge, Massachusetts: Alice James Books, 1992.

Lum, Wing Tek. *Expouding the Doubtful Points*. Honolulu: Bamboo Ridge Press, 1987.

Mar, Laureen. *Living Furniture*. Noro Press, 1982.

Mariano, Bayani Ligat. *Selected Poems*. Healdsburg, CA: Ya-Ka-Ama Indian Education and Development, [1977].

Matsueda, Pat. *The Fish Catcher*. Honolulu: Petronium Press, 1985.

McFerrin, Linda Watanabe. *The Impossiblity of Redemption Is Something We Hadn't Figured On*. Berkeley:

Berkeley Poets Workshop & Press, 1990.

Mirikitani, Janice. *Awake in the River*. San Francisco: Isthmus Press, 1978.

Mirikitani, Janice. *Shedding Silence*. California: Celestial Arts, 1987.

Mitsui, James [Masao]. *After the Long Train*. Minneapolis: Bieler Press, 1985.

Mitsui, James Masao. *Crossing the Phantom River*. Port Townsend, Washington: The Greywolf Press, 1978.

Mitsui, James Masao. *Journal of the Sun*. Port Townsend, Washington: Copper Canyon Press, 1974.

Mura, David. *After We Lost Our Way*. New York: E.P. Dutton, 1989.

Mura, David. *The Colors of Desire*. New York: Anchor, 1995.

Namjoshi, Suniti. *Cyclone in Pakistan*. Calcutta: Writers Workshop, 1971.

Namjoshi, Suniti. *The Jackass and the Lady*. Calcutta: Writers Workshop, 1980.

Namjoshi, Suniti. *More Poems*. Calcutta: Writers Workshop, 1970.

Namjoshi, Suniti. *Poems*. Calcutta: Writers Workshop, 1967.

Nguyen Long. *Tho con duong Mau & Nuoc Mat: The Road of Blood & Tears*. Santa Ana, CA: privately printed, 1981.

Nishizaki, Robert Kiyoshi. *Mongolian Blue*. Middle Water Press, 1978.

Noda, Barbara. *Strawberries*. San Francisco: Shameless Hussy Press, 1979.

Noguchi, Yone. *From the Eastern Shore*. New York: Kennerley, 1910.

Noguchi, Yone. *The Ganges Call Me*. Tokyo: Kyofunkwan, 1938.

Noguchi, Yone. *Japanese Hokkus*. Boston: Four Seas, 1920.

Noguchi, Yone. *Noguchi's Song Unto Brother Americans*. Oakland, CA.: 1897

Noguchi, Yone. *The Pilgrimage*. Kamakura, Japan: Valley Press, 1909.

Noguchi, Yone. *Seen and Unseen*. New York: Orientalia; San Francisco: G. Burgess & P.Garnett, 1897.

Noguchi, Yone. *The Selected Poems of Yone Noguchi*. Boston: Four Seas, 1921.

Noguchi, Yone. *The Summer Cloud*. Tokyo: Shunyodo, 1906.

Noguchi, Yone. *These Scattered Flowers of My Poetry*. Privately printed, N.d.

Noguchi, Yone. *The Voice of the Valley*. San Francisco: W. Doxey, 1897.

Oka, Francis Naohiko. *Poems: Memorial Edition*. San Francisco: City Lights, 1970.

Okita, Dwight. *Crossing with the Light*. Chicago: Tia Chucha Press, 1992.

Ondaatje, Michael. *The Concessions*. Blyth, ON: M. Ondaatje, 1982.

Ondaatje, Michael. *The Dainty Monsters*. Toronto: Coach House, 1967.

Ondaatje, Michael. *Elimination Dance*. Ilderton, ON: Nairn Coldstream, 1978

Ondaatje, Michael. *The Man with Seven Toes*. 1969. Toronto: Coach House, 1971.

Ondaatje, Michael. *"Rat Jelly" and Other Poems*. Toronto: Coach House Press, 1973.

Ondaatje, Michael. *There's a Trick with a Knife I'm Learning to Do*. New York: W.W. Norton and Company, 1979.

Ondaatje, Michael. *Secular Love*. New York: Norton, 1985.

Ondaatje, Michael. *Tin Roof*. Lantzville, BC: Island Writing Series, 1982.

Padmanab, S. *Ages of Birds*. Calcutta: Writers Workshop, 1976.

Padmanab, S. *A Separate Life*. Calcutta: Writers Workshop, 1974.

Padmanab, S. *Songs of the Slave*. Cornwall, ON: Vesta, 1977.

Parameswaran, Uma. *Cyclic Hope, Cyclic Pain*. Calcutta: Writers Workshop, 1973.

Parameswaran, Uma. *Trishanku*. Toronto: TSAR; Madras: East-west Press, 1988.

Rajan, Balachandra. "Monsoon." Cambridge: n.p., 1943.

Rajan, Tilottama. *Myth in a Metal Mirror*. Calcutta: Writers Workshop, 1967.

Ramanujan, A.K. *Relations*. London: Oxford University Press, 1971.

Ramanujan, A.K. *Selected Poems*. Delhi: Oxford University Press, 1976.

Ramanujan, A.K. *The Striders*. London: Oxford University Press, 1967.

Rampuri, Jeewan, and Robert Sward. *Cheers for Muktananda*. Victoria, BC: Soft Press, 1976.

Rasha, Mittar. *Murmurs*. Cornwall, On: Vesta, 1979.

Ravi, Ravinder. *Restless Soul*. Surrety, BC: Indo Canada Publishers, 1978.

Ravi, Ravinder. *Wind Song*. Surrey, BC: Indo Canada Publishers, 1980.

Reyes, Myrna Pena. *The River Singing Stone*. Oregon: Pacific House, 1983.

Robles, Al. *Kayaomunggi Vision of a Wandering Carabao*. San Francisco: Isthmus Foundation, 1983.

Robles, Al. *Rappin' with Ten Thousand Carabaos in the Dark*. Los Angeles: UCLA Asian American Studies Center, 1996.

Sabasu, Irare. *Poems in Unmasked*. Brooklyn: Fordham University, 1980

Sakaki, Nanao. *Bellyfulls*. Eugene, OR: Toad Press, 1966.

Sakaki, Nano. *Real Play: Poetry and Drama*. San Juan Pueblo, NM: Tooth of Time Books, 1983.

Sasaki, Yasuo. *Ascension*. Pasadena: Balconet Press, 1968.

San Juan, E. Jr. *The Ashes of Pedro Abad Santos*. Mansfield Depot CT: Phillipines Research Center, 1985.

San Juan, E. Jr. *The Exorcism*. Manila: Panitkan Publications, 1967.

San Juan, E. Jr. *Godkissing Carrion*. Cambridge, MA.: Concord Press, 1964.

Santos, Bienvenido. *Distances: In Time*. Manila: Ateneo De Manila University Press, 1983.

Santos, Bienvenido. *The Wounded Stag*. Manila: Capitol Publishing House, 1956.

Seth, Vikram. *The Golden Gate: A Novel in Verse*. New York: Random, 1986.

Seth, Vikram. *The Humble Administrator's Garden*. Manchester: Carcanet, 1985.

Sharma, P.D. *The New Caribbean Man*. Hayward, CA: Carib House, 1981.

Shikatani, Gerry. *A Sparrow's Food*. Toronto: Coach House Press, 1984.

Shikatani, Gerry. *Barking of Dog*. Toronto: Missing Link Press, 1973.

Shikatani, Gerry. *Haliburton*. Toronto: Missing Link Press, 1975.

Shikatani, Gerry. *1988: Selected Poems and Texts/Nineteen Seventy Three*. Toronto: Underwhich Editions, 1987.

Shikatani, Gerry. *Ship Sands Island*. Toronto: Gangalia Press, 1978.

Shiraishi, Kazuko. *Seasons of Sacred Lust*. New York: New Directions, 1978.

Singh, Nirmala. *The Shiva Dance*. Cornwall, ON: Vesta, 1979.

Song, Cathy. *Picture Bride*. New Haven: Yale Univ. Press, 1983.

Song, Cathy. *Frameless Windows, Squares of Light*. New York: W.W. Norton and Co., 1988.

Song, Cathy. *School Figures*. Pittsburgh: University of Pittsburgh Press, 1994.

Sze, Arthur. *Archipelago*. Port Townsend, WA: Copper Canyon Press, 1995.

Sze, Arthur. *Dazzled*. California: Floating Island Publications, 1982.

Sze, Arthur. *River River*. Providence: Lost Roads Publishers, 1987.

Sze, Arthur. *The Willow Wind*. Santa Fe: Tooth of Time, 1981.

Sze, Arthur. *Two Ravens*. Santa Fe: Tooth of Time, 1976.

Tagami, Jeff. *October Light*. San Francisco: Kearny Street Workshop, 1987.

Tanaka, Ronald. *The Shino Suite*. New York: Greenfield Review Press, 1982.

Thich Nhat-Hanh. *The Cry of Vietnam*. Trans. author with Helen Coutant. Drawings by Vo Dinh. Santa Barbara, CA: Unicorn Press, 1968.

Thich Nhat-Hanh. *The Viet Nam*. Santa Barbara, CA: Unicorn Press, 1967.

Thich Nhat-Hanh. *Zen Poems*. Trans. teo Savory. Greensboro, NC: Unicorn Press, 1976.

Ting, Walasse. *Chinese Moonlight*. New York: Wittenborn, 1967.

Ting, Walasse. *Hot and Sour Soup*. N.p.: Sam Francis Foundation, 1969.

Ting, Walasse. *My Shit and My Love*. Bruxelles: Galerie Smith, 1961.

Ting, Walasse. *1{cent} Life*. Ed. Sam Francis. Bern: E.W. Kornfield, 1964.

Tsiang, H.T. *Poems of Chinese Revolution*. New York: Privately Printed, 1929.

Trask, Haunani-Kay. *Light in the Crevice Never Seen*. Corvallis, OR: Calyx Books, 1994.

Tsuda, Margaret. *Cry Love Aloud*. New York: Poetica Press, 1972.

Tsuda, Margaret. *Urban River*. Newark, NJ: Discovery Books, 1976.

Tsui, Kitty. *The Words of a Woman Who Breathes Fire*. San Francisco: Spinsters Ink, 1983.

Uyematsu, Amy. *30 Miles from J-Town*. Brownsville, OR: Story Line Press, 1992.

Vien, Minh. Saigon: *The Unhealed Wound*. San Francisco: Moonlit Garden, 1990.

Villa, Jose Garcia. *Appassionata: Poems in Praise of Love*. New York: King & Cowen, 1979.

Villa, Jose Garcia. *Have Come Am Here*. New York: Viking, 1942.

Villa, Jose Garcia. *Makata 3*. Manila: Alberto S. Florentino, 1973.

Villa, Jose Garcia. *Many Voices*. Manila: Phillipine Book Guild, 1939.

Villa, Jose Garcia. *Seven Poems*. Cambridge, Mass.: Wake, 1948.

Villa, Jose Garcia. *Volume Two*. New York: New Directions, 1949.

Villa, Jose Garcia. *Selected Poems and New*. New York: McDowell, Oblensky, 1958.

Viray, Manuel A. *After This Exile*. Quezon City, Philippines: Phoenix Publishing House, 1965.

Viray, Manuel A. *Where Blood with Light Collides*. Manila: privately printed, 1975.

Wah, Fred. *Alley Alley Home Free*. Red Deer, Alberta: Red Deer College Press, 1992.

Wah, Fred. *Among*. Toronto: Coach House Press, 1972.

Wah, Fred. *Breathin' My Name with a Sigh*. Vancouver: Talonbooks, 1981.

Wah, Fred. *Earth*. Canton, NY: Inst. of Further Studies, 1974.

Wah, Fred. *Grasp the Sparrow's Tail*. Kyoto, 1982.

Wah, Fred. *Lardeau*. Toronto: Island Press, 1965.

Wah, Fred. *Limestone Lakes Utaniki*. Red Deer, Alberta: Red Deer College Press, 1989.

Wah, Fred. *Loki is Buried at Smokey Creek: Selected Poems*. Vancouver: Talonbooks, 1980.

Wah, Fred. *Mountain*. Buffalo, NY: Audit, 1967.

Wah, Fred. *Music at the Heart of Thinking*. Red Deer, Alberta: Red Deer College Press, 1987.

Wah, Fred. *Owner's Manual*. Lantzville, BC: Island Writing Series, 1981.

Wah, Fred. *Pictograms from the Interior of B.C.* Vancouver: Talonbooks, 1975.

Wah, Fred. *Rooftops*. South Harpswell, ME: Blackberry— Salted in the Shell, 1987.

Wah, Fred. *So Far*. Vancouver: Talonbooks, 1991.

Wah, Fred. *Tree*. Vancouver: Vancouver Community Press, 1972.

Wah, Fred. *Waiting for Saskatchewan*. Winnipeg: Turnstone, 1985.

Wang, David Rafael. *The Goblet Moon*. Vermont: Steinhaur Press, 1955.

Wang, David Rafael. *The Intercourse*. New York: Greenfield Review Press, 1974.

Wang, David Rafael. *Rivers on Fire*. Dunkirk, New York: Basilisk Press, 1974–75.

Wang, Yun. *The Carp*. Jamaica, VT: Bull Thistle Press, 1994.

Weerasinghe, Asoka. *Exile*. Cornwall, ON: Vesta, 1978.

Weerasinghe, Asoka. *Home Again Lanka*. Ottawa: Commoner's, 1981.

Weerasinghe, Asoka. *Hot Tea and Cinnamon Buns*. Cornwall, ON: Vesta, 1980.

Weerasinghe, Asoka. *Poems for Jeannie*. Cornwall, ON: Vesta, 1976.

Weerasinghe, Asoka. *Poems in November*. Ottawa: Commoner's, 1977.

Weerasinghe, Asoka. *Selected Poems* (1958–83). Cornwall, ON: Vesta, 1983.

Wong, May. *A Bad Girl's Book of Animals*. New York: Harcourt Brace Jovanovich, 1974.

Wong, May. *Reports*. New York: Harcourt Brace, 1970.

Wong, May. *Superstitions*. New York: Harcourt Brace Jovanovich, 1978.

Wong, Nanying Stella. *Man Curving to Sky*. San Francisco: Anthelion Press, 1976.

Wong, Nellie. *Dreams in Harrison Railroad Park*. California: Kelsey St. Press, 1977.

Wong, Nellie. *The Death of Long Steam Lady*. Los Angeles: West End Press, 1986.

Yamada, Mitsuye. *Camp Notes*. San Francisco: Shameless Hussy Press, 1976.

Yamada, Mitsuye. *Desert Run*. Lantham, New York: Kitchen Table/Women of Color Press, 1988.

Yasuda, Kenneth [under pseud. Shosun]. *A Pepper-Pod: Classic Japanese Poems together with Original Haiku*. New York: Knopf, 1947.

Yau, John. *Broken Off By the Music*. St.Paul, MN.: Burning Deck, 1981.

Yau, John. *Corpse and Mirror*. New York: Holt Reinhart and Winston, 1983.

Yau, John. *Crossing Canal Street*. New York: The Bellevue Press, 1976.

Yau, John. *Edificio Sayonara*. Santa Rosa, CA.: Black Sparrow Press, 1992.

Yau, John. *Notarikon*. New York: Jordan Davies, 1981.

Yau, John. *Radiant Silhouette: New and Selected Work 1974–1988*. Santa Rosa, CA.: Black Sparrow Press, 1989.

Yau, John. *The Reading of an Ever-changing Tale*. New York: Nobodaddy Press, 1977.

Yau, John. *The Sleepless Night of Eugene Delacroix*. Berkeley: Release Press, 1980.

Yau, John. *Sometimes*. New York: The Sheep Meadow Press, 1979.

Yoon, Jean. *Under a Hostile Moon*. Toronto: Two Bits Press, 1993.

Yup, Paula. *Love Poems*. East Talmouth, MA: Peka Boo Press, 1984.

zarco, cyn. *cir'cum.nav'i.ga'tion*. Santa Fe: Tooth of Time, 1986.

ANTHOLOGIES

Asian Women United, ed. *Ikon 9* (1988).

Balaz, Joseph P., ed. *Ho'omanoa: An Anthology of Contemporary Hawaiian Literature*. Honolulu: Ku Pa'a Incorporated, 1989.

Bay Area Pilipino American Writers, ed. *Without Names: A Collection of Poems*. San Francisco: Kearny Street Workshop Press, 1985.

Bruchac, Joseph, ed. *Breaking Silence: An Anthology of Contemporary Asian American Poets*. Greenfield Center: Greenfield Review Press, 1983.

Cachapero, Emily, et. al., eds. *Liwanag: Literary and Graphic Expression by Filipinos in America*. San Francisco: Liwanag Publications, 1975.

Chiang, Fay, et. al., eds. *American Born and Foreign: An Anthology of Asian American Poetry*. New York: Sunbury Press Books, 1979.

Chock, Eric, and Darrell H. Y. Lum, eds. *The Best of Bamboo Ridge: The Hawaii Writers' Quarterly*. Honolulu: Bamboo Ridge Press, 1986.

Chung, C., et. al., ed. *Between the Lines: An Anthology of Pacific/Asian Lesbians of Santa Cruz, California*. Santa Cruz: Dancing Bird Press, 1987.

Fisher, Dexter, ed. *The Third Woman: Minority Women Writers of the United States*. Boston: Houghton, 1980.

Gee, Emma, ed. *Counterpoint: Asian American Perspectives*. Los Angeles: Asian American Studies Center, University of California, 1976.

Gill, Stephen, ed. *Green Snow: Anthology of Canadian Poets of Asian Origin*. Cornwall, ON: Vesta Publications, 1976.

Hamasaki, Richard, ed. *Seaweeds and Constructions: Anthology Hawaii*. Honolulu, 1979.

Hiura, Jerrold Asao, ed. *The Hawk's Well: A Collection of Japanese American Art and Literature*. San Jose, CA: Asian American Art Projects, 1986.

Hongo, Garrett, ed. *The Open Boat: Poems from Asian America*. New York: Anchor, 1992.

Hongo, Garrett Kaoru, ed. *Greenfield Review* 6.1-2 (1977).

Hom, Marlon K., ed. and trans. *Songs of Gold Mountain: Cantonese Rhymes from San Francisco Chinatown*. Berkeley: University of California Press, 1987.

Hsu, Kai-yu and Helen Palubinskas, ed. *Asian-American Authors*. Boston: Houghton Mifflin, 1972.

Kalsey, Surjeet, ed. *Contemporary Literature in Translation* [Mission, BC] 26 (1977).

Kudaka, Geraldine, ed. *On a Bed of Rice: An Asian American Erotic Feast*. New York: Anchor, 1995.

Lai, Him Mark, Genny Lim, and Judy Yung, eds. and trans. *Island: Poetry and History of Chinese Immigrants on Angel Island, 1910-1940*. San Francisco: HOC DOI, 1980.

Legaspi, Joaquin. *Joaquin Legaspi: Poet, Artist, Community Worker*. Comp. Jovina Navarro. El Verano, CA: Pilnachi Press, 1976.

Lew, Walter K., ed. *Premonitions: The Kaya Anthology of New*

Asian North American Poetry. New York: Kaya Production, 1995.

Lim, Shirley Geok-lin and Mayumi Tsutukawa ed. *The Forbidden Stitch: An Asian American Women's Anthology*. Corvallis, OR: Calyx Books, 1989.

Lim-Hing, Sharon, ed. *The Very Inside: An Anthology of Writing by Asian and Pacific Islander Lesbian and Bisexual Women*. Toronto: Sister Vision Press, 1994.

Mar, Laureen and Alan Chong Lau, ed. *Contact/II* 7.38-40 (Winter/Spring 1986).

Mirikitani et. al., ed. *Ayumi: A Japanese American Anthology*. San Francisco: The Japanese American Anthology Committee, 1980.

Mirikitani, et. al., ed. *Time to Greez! Incantations from the Third World*. San Francisco: Glide Publications, 1975.

Nakano, Jiro and Kay Nakano, ed. and trans. *Poets Behind Barbed Wire*. Honolulu: Bamboo Ridge Press, 1983.

Nishimura, Tomi and Chusaburo Ito, ed. *Maple: Tanka Poems by Japanese Canadians*. Trans. Toyoshi Hiramatsu. Toronto: Continental Times, 1975.

Nixon, Lucille M., and Tomoe Tana, trans. *Sounds from the Unknown: A Collection of Japanese-American Tanka*. Denver: Alan Swallow, 1963.

Okinawa Club of America. *History of the Okinawans in North America*. trans. Ben Kobashigawa. Los Angeles: Okinawa Club of America and Asian American Studies Center, University of California, 1988.

Okutsu, James K., project director. *Fusion '83: A Japanese American Anthology*. San Francisco: Asian American Studies Dept., San Francisco State University, 1984.

Okutsu, James K., project director. *Fusion-San*. San Francisco: Asian American Studies Dept., San Francisco State University, 1986.

Okutsu, James K., project director. *Fusion Too: A Japanese American Anthology*. San Francisco: Asian American

Studies Dept., San Francisco State University, 1985.

Reed, Ishmael, ed. *CALAFIA: The California Poetry.* Berkeley: Y'Bird Books, 1979.

Shikitani, Gerry and David Aylward, ed. *Paper Doors: An Anthology of Japanese Canadian Poetry.* Toronto: Coach House Press, 1981.

Stewart, Frank, and John Unterecker, eds. *Poetry Hawaii: A Contemporary Anthology.* Honolulu: University of Hawaii Press, 1979.

Sunoo, Brenda Paik, ed. *Korean American Writings.* New York: Insight, 1975.

Tachiki, Amy, et. al., ed. *Roots: An Asian American Reader.* Los Angeles: Continental Graphics, 1971.

Third World Women. San Francisco: Third World Communications, 1972.

Tsutakawa, Mayumi, and Alan Chong Lau, ed. *Turning Shadows into Light: Art and Culture of the Northwest's Early Asian/Pacific Community.* Seattle: Young Pine, 1982.

Wand, David Hsin-fu, ed. *Asian American Heritage: An Anthology of Poetry and Prose.* New York: Washington Square Press, 1974.

Wang, L. Ling-chi and Henry Zhao, ed. *Chinese American Poetry: An Anthology.* Santa Barbara: Asian American Voices, 1991.

We Won't Move: Poems and Photographs of the International Hotel Struggle. San Francisco: Kearny Street Workshop Press, 1977.

Wong, Shawn, and Frank Chin, ed. *Yardbird Reader* 4 (1974).

Yellow Pearl. New York: Basement Workshop, 1972.

Yoisho! An Anthology of the Japantown Arts and Media Workshop. San Francisco: Japantown Art and Media Workshop, 1983.

160

Sojin Takei: "Untitled", translated by Jiro and Kay Nakano, reprinted from *Poets Behind Barbed Wire* (Bamboo Ridge Press, 1983) by permission of Judy Nasu. Copyright © 1983 by Sojin Takei.

H.T. Tsiang: "Chinaman, Laundryman", "Rickshaw Boy", and "Shantung" reprinted from *Poems of the Chinese Revolution* (privately printed, 1929). Copyright © 1929 by H.T. Tsiang. "He was Satirizing" reprinted from *The Hanging on Union Square* (privately printed, 1935). Copyright © 1935 by H.T. Tsiang.

Jose Garcia Villa: "57" reprinted from *Have Come. Am Here* (Viking Press, 1942) by permission of the poet and his agent, John Cowen. Copyright © 1942 by Jose Garcia Villa. "Untitled ('When, I')" reprinted from *Poems 55* (Alberto S. Florentino, 1962) by permission of the poet and his agent. Copyright © 1962 by Jose Garcia Villa.

Fred Wah: "They are Burning" originally from *Lardeau* (Island Press, 1965) and reprinted from *Loki is Buried at Smoky Creek: Selected Poems* (Talonbooks, 1980) by permission of the poet. Copyright © 1980 by Fred Wah. "Mountain" originally from *Mountain* (Audit, 1967) and reprinted from *Loki is Buried at Smoky Creek: Selected Poems* (Talonbooks, 1980) by permission of the poet. Copyright © 1980 by Fred Wah.

Wen I-to: "The Laundry Song" reprinted from *Asian American Journey* (1981) and *Twentieth Century Chinese Poetry* (Cornell University Press, 1963). Copyright © 1963 by Wen I-to.

Wong May: "Spring Comes to Kresge Co." and "Bastard" reprinted from *A Bad Girl's Book of Animals* (Harcourt Brace & World, Inc., 1968) by permission of Harcourt Brace, & Co. Copyright © 1968 by Wong May.

Hisaye Yamamoto: "Et Ego In America VIXI" and

ABOUT THE EDITOR

Juliana Chang is Assistant Professor of English at Boston College. She is currently working on a book-length study of Asian American poetry.